MYSTIC MASQUERADE
An Adoptee's Search for Truth

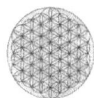

VALERIE NAIMAN

A SPIRITED PRESS BOOK

Edited by Lydia McClaren
Cover design by Mylinda Bryant
Art design by Valerie Naiman and Mylinda Bryant
Photography by Julius Naiman, Valerie Naiman and Toni Brost

This story is true, except for a few name changes to protect the identity
of the not-so-innocent.

ISBN: 979-8-9881475-0-3 (paperback)
ISBN: 979-8-9881475-1-0 (ebook)
ISBN: 979-8-9881475-2-7 (audiobook expanded)

Printed in the United States of America on
Forest Stewarded acid-free paper.

There are only two mistakes
one can make
along the road to truth:

not going all the way,
and not starting.

Buddha

CONTENTS

PART 4 MISSING LINKS

PART 5 MASQUERADE

INTRO

Except for a few enlightened beings, we all lose our identity when birthed into the world. Having mine erased twice before I was seven led me on a mysterious lifelong journey. My search went beyond discovering who I am into a deeper exploration of who we all are and where we came from.

We each play a part in this life drama with our various masks and costumes. Eventually, self-inquiry arises, and we ask 'Who am I?'' What's the purpose and mission of my life? Unveiling that truth is a mystical masquerade that takes an inquisitive mind that thinks beyond the norm.

I invite you to travel with me through the uncharted terrain I tread. My sincere wish is that this book inspires your own profound journey of knowingness. Whether you are an adoptee or not, traversing the enigma of identity can lead you to your authentic self.

> *"If you would be a real seeker of truth,*
> *it is necessary that at least once in your life*
> *you doubt, as far as possible, all things."*
> *~ Rene Descartes*

Connect with me at *valerienaiman.com* to hear story songs, podcasts, listen to parts of the expanded audiobook, and download freebies.

Photos of some of some of the scenes in this book are available. Send requests to: valerie@valerienaiman.com

PART 1
SELFDOM

1

MYTHS

I was taken from my mother's womb at birth, never to see her again. Un-held, I entered a frigid black hole with no compass. As an infant, there was no way to grasp what had happened. Life catapulted me into an abyss of mystery that took decades to unravel.

As I write this, it's fitting that I'm cruising on a ship over the mysterious Bermuda Triangle. The parting of clouds gifts my keyboard with a glimmer of the sun's rays beckoning me to share the route I traveled. Only now that I've found my bearings am I able to share my story.

From an early age, seeking the truth became my modus vivendi. I lost myself many times along the way as I solved one mystery after another. Today I've emerged with an understanding of my life and the initial birth trauma. In adoptee land, some call it 'coming out of the fog.' For others, we can call it 'coming into a state of soul awareness.'

I begin the story at age seven.

The Aviary Surprise

I never fit in and spent lots of time pretending I was a singing, dancing canary. We had a huge aviary for our flock of white canaries, and my daily ritual was bringing them water to bathe in. They were always chipper and sang when I came in. I'd make up my own trilling melodies, and they'd mimic me back. I loved how they fluttered in the water and shook it off like they were dancing.

One day, during our chirping concerto, my brother Lee came in, ticked off about something. He was my antagonist, and I was an easy target, being three years younger. His face was boiling red as he threw his baseball cap onto the dirt floor and kicked up dust. "What's wrong?" I asked.

Lee yelled out, "We don't belong here!" He stormed out slamming the door, mumbling, "They're not our parents!"

There wasn't a peep in the birdhouse. They're not our parents? There's a lot I don't remember about my youth, but that moment is permanently carved into my being.

I didn't know what caused Lee's outburst. Was he just being mean? I found Mom and Dad inside sitting at our large antique walnut dining room table. Staring at them, I wondered if my brother had lied to me. I sure didn't look like them. My blonde hair and blue eyes were nowhere to be seen in my entire family. I wondered why my parents were so much older than my friends' parents. It began to sink in that it might be true.

I looked up at the antique chandelier as memories of stories I'd heard about my birth rushed forth. Had I really swung on it years ago and broken it? If it were true that they weren't my parents, would they send me away? Scared stiff, I stared at Daddy as he wrote something in his leather-bound notebook.

Mom saw my distraught state and asked if I wanted some ice cream. That was the go-to when we were unhappy about something. "No!" I screamed. Daddy looked up and asked what was wrong. I had to know now, right now. With the tact of a tattletale, I squealed, "Lee says you're not our real parents."

They looked at each other with deadpan faces but didn't say a word. The only sound in the room was me wiping sniffles on my shirt. It was Daddy who broke the stifling silence. He cleared his throat and announced, "We will not discuss this." They were my parents, he said, and that was that. After all they had done for me, why would I ever doubt them?

I ran up the stairs to my room as my heart pounded harder with each step. They denied it, but the queasiness in my stomach knew something was wrong. Jumping into my bed fort, my rampant imagination plummeted into darkness. Multitudes of questions suffocated me. Who were my parents? Was I given away? Who could tell me the truth? Did I have a sister out there ... or a big family? Gasping for breath, my trembling fingers grabbed Sissy, my sock monkey. Being my confidant, I interrogated her with questions. Holding Sissy tighter and tighter, I began choking her for answers until I slung her across the room.

The maid came up saying she'd brought me dinner and set it at my door. I was only hungry for the truth. I wrangled with myself under my sheets until I fell asleep clutching my tear-soaked pillow.

When I awoke, I saw Sissy had landed across the room on wooden Dutch clogs I'd gotten on my last birthday. Was I Dutch? Was that supposed to be a clue? It was overwhelming to figure all this out on my own. They'd made it clear not to talk about it, and I didn't want to hurt them. After all, it seemed like I owed them my life.

A knock on the door interrupted my growling stomach. It was the maid making sure I'd heard the breakfast bell. I peeked around the door as she picked up the untouched dinner tray. She raised her eyebrows in disapproval, giving me the once-over. "I'll be down soon," I said.

When my parent's cars were gone, I tiptoed down each creaky wooden step hoping not to see anyone. My gloomy thoughts were too horrid to talk to anyone about. My life was about to go haywire.

Mystery Birth

The story of how I came into being was altogether different from the stork scenario. I was fabled to be from a tribe of monkeys. Even though what I was told was a lie, it made me believe I could dance better than any of my friends. I always thought there was a gift somewhere in our life's catastrophes, and that was one of mine.

On family outings, we'd often go to "The Monkey Jungle" in Miami so I could see my ancestors. My parents said they brought me home from there because I was so cute. Mom said my extraordinarily long fingers were unique, and I could do things most kids couldn't do. They often took me to visit my monkey tribe, where I loved watching their acrobatic antics as they swung through the tree branches.

When I asked what had happened to my tail, they said they were sorry. They'd cut it off because I'd hang from the chandelier in our dining room, and they didn't want me to get hurt. I actually became an awesome acrobatic swinger, and later my long fingers proved excellent for piano. Taking after my tribe, I became a fearless uncontrollable child. Most of my girlfriends had dolls, but not me. I had an array of sock monkeys. Sissy was my best friend for decades until I gave her up for adoption years later to my friend's daughter.

2

DANCING IN
AND OUT OF
CHARACTER

My father's sister, my Aunt Lilly, came to visit and I asked her if I was adopted. She only told me my mother couldn't have more children. She said I was a dream come true for my parents, and I needed to do anything to make them happy. That was a big task to lay on a kid.

My Parents?

My Dad, Julius Naiman, graduated law school at 18 by lying for years about his age. His mother let him get away with it if he kept his grades up. His great-grandfather was one of the first rabbis in New York, but not liking organized religion, Dad jumped ship from that family tradition and set off on his own after college.

In 1918, he moved to Florida's small village of Coconut Grove and landed a job as the town's first city commissioner.

At that time, there were no paved roads and part of his position was to design a transport plan for the town. What developed is still there today and has kept the town charmingly unique. The streets wind about and are named after birds, flowers, and trees. Dad was a naturalist at heart and taught me to appreciate the beauty of the world.

Back in Maryland, he'd been a top-notch tennis player. It disheartened him to discover there were no courts in the Grove. He built a tennis court behind Town Hall to solve this problem. But when he ordered their first fire truck, there was nowhere to park it. It was either take out the tennis court or get a smaller fire truck. That was a no-brainer for Dad. He traded the fancy new big fire truck for an older, smaller one from Miami.

Dad had a colorful variety of careers. He opened one of the first speakeasy clubs in Miami, called the Tropicana Nightclub. When he interviewed the Marx Brothers for an act, he said they had promise but weren't ready yet. Humor was the deepest connection I had with Dad. He taught me to find the light side of things. He was adept at keeping secrets as he served in Army intelligence in World War I and II. Later, he became a private detective. I know that because I found his detective badge and asked him about it. He said he couldn't tell me about that time in his life. Dad was also a 33rd-degree Mason in a secret society. He never told me what it meant when he waved his handkerchief and did other peculiar things. Isn't it odd that Masons swear a vow to Truth yet have all kinds of secret signals so others don't understand them?

I was wary of secrets and investigated anything held back from me. I'd even test my friends, and if someone lied, that was the end of the friendship. It wasn't even a conscious connection back then. I became a spy like I imagined Daddy was. I took after him because I wanted so bad to fit in.

We had a big poker room where Dad's buddies came every Friday night. Sometimes I'd watch from my bedroom window as suited-up men approached the house. If I hadn't gone to my room yet, they inevitably bowed, took off their fedora hats, and waved them across their chests on their way to the secret room. The poker room was off-limits to us kids, but the waft of cigar smoke permeated the air up into my bedroom. Sometimes, I'd sneak down to the breakfast room door and peek through the keyhole to see what they were doing. I once heard Dad telling them he'd eaten off gold plates at Al Capone's house in Miami Beach when he was a detective.

My parents waited until late in life to do the family thing. They bought a big house, started a family with my brother Lee and then me three years later. Then Dad opened another business called Tropicana Publishers for his books and magazines. I sure wish he had copyrighted the word "Tropicana" because I'd be a gazillionaire today.

Dad was an avid writer and was honored in Congress three times with Freedom Foundation awards. He bought me journals, taught me to type, and always wanted me to be a writer.

Being adventurous and fun-loving, Dad would tap quietly on my bedroom door before daybreak and whisper, "Let's sneak out and tell stories." We'd quietly leave for breakfast like prowling cats in the dark. Later in life, he'd take me out with my friends and play the getaway driver while we'd jump out and wrap someone's house in toilet paper. It was a thing back then.

Mom's maiden name was Houghtaling. Her family had the first health food store in Miami. She gave me homeopathic medicines, which Dad scoffed at. She was a smart cookie and was the first woman to graduate with a business degree from the University of Miami. Dad sought her out to work for him, and they became partners in business, then for life. As Dad's counterpart, she became the Worthy Matron head of the Eastern Star, the feminine aspect of the Masons. She was also the chairperson of the Women's Democratic Club and became a delegate to the Democratic National Convention. Mom wasn't shy and quickly found herself in leadership roles. She had minored in theater in college and it showed. She loved dressing me up, taking me to events, and showing me off. There were rarely any kids at these events since Mom's friends were all older. But on the bright side, I learned a lot from adults instead.

Mom was a non-stop go-getter, and she wanted the same for me. I learned how to manifest by observing her. She taught me that following a dream is all part of manifestation. She imbued in me the gift of knowing how powerful we can be if we don't doubt ourselves.

With her love of theater arts, she was a natural stage mother. By age three, I was performing all kinds of skits and acrobatics. Dad told her I could imitate anybody because I had an excellent monkey mind. Once a week we'd go to one of the Jewish delis on Miami Beach, where they cleared off a table, set me on top, and I'd tap dance. My reward was gefilte fish, borscht, and my favorite smashed banana with honey halva.

Mom entered me in all sorts of contests and pageants. Life became an endless journey of Easter Parades and Little Miss Whatnots. When I wasn't busy entertaining, Mom sent me off to a score of classes. Learning piano, tap, ballet, acrobatics, and baton kept me on the run. I was Mom's Shirley Temple and I wanted to please her. Fortunately, I wasn't shy. After all, my monkey tribe in the jungle certainly wasn't.

Later, in my cheerleader phase, she sent me to cotillion dance classes. Her final attempt to civilize me was sending me to charm school to learn social etiquette. I had a good life, developing loads of skills, but the social skills part never took hold. By high school, the theater became my avenue of expression. I could be anyone I wanted to be. I didn't know who I was, so I just made it up as I went.

Sometimes I'd skip school and go people-watching to develop new characters. I was also curious why there are so many religions and ideologies in the world. Some of my hooky time involved sneaking into different temples, churches, and synagogues. Did any of them know the truth about our origins? The more I realized that no one knew, the more I wanted to know.

Leaving Home

Being overly protected at home, I became rebellious. None of my friends had babysitters, and I felt ridiculous having one as a teenager. Much to my parent's chagrin, I ran away from home in tenth grade. I moved in with my girlfriend Susan and her family. We had been friends as cheerleaders and kind of looked alike. We both loved our theater thespian life at Miami High. That was the only thing I liked about school. I got to play roles and pretend to be somebody else. People thought we were sisters, and we played along with it. Susan being the calm rational one, tamed my wild side to keep us out of trouble. Upon graduation, she married her high school boyfriend, and I landed a job doing summer stock theater.

My job took me to an amphitheater show called Horn in the West in Boone, North Carolina. I had three roles to perform, which all required acting, singing, and dancing. My first role was as a pioneer. Then, I'd run to the dressing room, strip down and rub what they called "Texas dirt" all over me to be an Indian. Then I'd shower off and slip into another pioneer costume to walk the Trail of Tears part of the play.

The cast and crew lived in an apartment building with three to four of us in each unit. I had three roommates, all older than me, and when it got too close for comfort, I decided to find a place to rent on my own and buy my first car.

I was already doing two shows a night: Horn in the West and a midnight show at the Powder Horn Theater. I got two more jobs, so I'd have enough money to be independent. In the morning, I cleaned rooms in a motel, and afternoons I did food prep in a restaurant. My workday began at daybreak and ended after midnight. Soon, I had enough money to rent a cheap cabin in the woods a few miles out of town. Then, I bought my first car for $500., a black 1950 push-button Rambler with questionable brakes. When she rolled herself across the main street and smashed into a building, I named her The Bitch.

Work kept me from enjoying my solo lifestyle, but taking care of myself was a major accomplishment. My independent persona became a badge of self-worth. I was out of character if I wasn't busy taking things into my own hands.

College Drama and Epilepsy

When summer stock ended, I returned home to attend college. My parents wanted to pay for my education, but I didn't want to be indebted to anyone for anything. Being independent kept a fire under my ass. My attitude might have been different if my parents told me about my adoption and gotten me some counseling.

Miami-Dade College had a superb theater program. The costumer, Ann Whitlock, became my mentor. She took me on as her final protégé so she could retire. Besides being a costumer extraordinaire, Ann was a mystic. Being curious about anything unknown, I pestered her with questions. She was the first person to introduce me to the occult. Ann became a dual mentor in costuming and metaphysics, and we spent many late nights delving into psychic phenomena.

One night, I cut my hand with sharp scissors and fell to the floor unconscious. I awoke to the smell of whiskey Ann poured on my head to revive me. I assured her I was okay and wanted to tell her about my visions before they slipped away.

She listened intently as she wrapped my left hand in white gauze. When I finished, Ann poured two whiskeys on the rocks. She toasted me for gaining insight into the other side. She said the visions proved that I wasn't unconscious and that humans are much more than the physical body.

The next day Ann bought me a book about a psychic named Edgar Cayce, who was a famous fainter. He'd go into a trance and receive visions for people who suffered from various diseases. I soaked the information up and kept asking for more.

Six months later, I pierced my right index finger with a sewing machine needle. This time, Ann saw me having a seizure. Even though she'd seen me faint before, I hadn't told anyone about my spells. Ever since I was old enough to walk, I'd fainted at the sight of blood or the smell of a doctor's office. Later in life, I realized this was related to my traumatic birth experience. Growing up my father took me to a doctor whenever I hurt myself in a minor way, despite my pleas that I didn't want to go.

In junior high, I had seizures, and doctors diagnosed me as an epileptic. When I began my menstrual cycle as a teenager, I fainted at that too. My brother Lee always yelled, "Hey, she's got it again!" He somehow found that humorous.

When doctors asked my mother about any family history of fainting, she was vague. It could have made a difference if my parents had been open about my adoption. Having one's genetic information stripped can cause serious mishaps. It's frustrating to continually be asked about medical history when you're clueless. It's not fair that adoptees don't come with some kind of bio-manual to help us and adopted parents traverse the medical maze.

I never trusted doctors and hid any sign of not feeling well for fear I'd be carried off to one. Sometimes I'd come to after a seizure, and if no one had seen me, I kept quiet. Biting my lip in secrecy had a new meaning for me. After numerous tests, no one knew why I had spells. They gave me pharmaceuticals and said I'd need to take medication for the rest of my life. At least I didn't have to keep going back for tests. Suspicious of anything a doctor gave me, I tucked the pills away.

When I came to after my seizure, Ann was hovering over me, calling my name. I'd only been out a minute, but it felt like eons, as usual. Catching a glimpse of blood, I turned away and raised my legs on a chair to get the blood back to my head and not pass out again. I asked Ann to find some smelling salts in my purse and assured her I was okay. She told me I had convulsed and we needed to get to a hospital. Panicked by the thought, I pleaded with her until she understood that a hospital would only make it worse.

Once I sniffed my way up to a sitting position, she calmed down. I assured her I was okay and hadn't wanted people to know I was a fainter, much less that I sometimes convulsed. To be more discreet in college, I kept my smelling salts in my purse instead of carrying them in a vial on a necklace. Ann insisted I wear it around my neck again to be closer at hand in an emergency. Plus, she said, she was running out of whiskey!

I'd been reading about Edgar Cayce's remedies and now delved deeper into his work. I made some of his elixirs, changed my diet, took steam baths, and got my first colonic. Whenever I got a chance, I'd bury myself in the sand at the beach. I never fainted or had a seizure for the rest of my college days. But the word was out that I was an epileptic. People acted differently after that ... it was like the way some people changed when I later knew I was adopted. That happens to adoptees a lot. There's a stigma attached to us. Are they thinking, "Oh, it's so sad that you weren't wanted," or "Oh, you must have felt abandoned!" People can say the dumbest things. How would I know how I felt as an infant?

Magic Keys

At the end of my last semester, Ann told me she'd taught me all she knew about costuming and was retiring. She said it was time for me to move on and gave me a set of what she called magical keys. Ann said they could unlock doors for my desired future. She said I could do whatever I wanted, but I needed to decide what that was. Although that sounded like some far-fetched monkey business, I was ready for a change. I told Ann I'd shoot for the stars.

I wanted to work on Broadway as an actress. Ann pulled a few strings and got me an audition for an off-Broadway show. That landed me a job with Touring Productions Inc. My role was a blonde bombshell lead in a musical called Whoops! Our rehearsal hall was on the top floor of the Ed Sullivan Theater on Broadway!

Most of the roles I played after that were the stereotyped ditzy blonde, but at least I got to sing. From there, I toured, performing in shows for a week to a month in various places. Every tour cast I joined included people who were into metaphysics. Between shows, we'd dive into the occult. I tried contacting my birth mother during a few seances with no success. We imagined she was still alive, and tarot cards also indicated that. We called ourselves the Touring Mystical Gypsies. I'll never forget us levitating peanuts and getting goofy, trying to use our minds to bend spoons.

Indulgences

After a year of touring, I got a scholarship to Florida State University and moved to Tallahassee. The theater department provided extraordinary growth opportunities for me. One highlight was when Lily Tomlin came as a visiting artist and shared some of her tricks of the trade with us. She said imagination is an actress's best tool and that she herself was primarily a figment of her imagination. That seemed right up my alley. Her comedy performances in Laugh-In always intrigued me, and I became her loyal fan.

I was cast as the understudy of a famous actress in the off-Broadway musical Halloween. I've never done as much partying as I did with these actors. Besides other indulgences, drinking was a daily routine. My parents never drank, so this was all new to me. I'll keep their names confidential, but I dove in and drank like a fish with them. I still wondered if I was adopted and imagined my mother was a drunken actress.

When the leading lady had a severe mishap from overindulging, I cleaned up my act and stepped into her role. The entire play occurred inside a mental ward, and it all felt so real.

My next indulgence proved to be better medicine for me. I took a pantomime class from a wild professor named Chuck. Our textbook was Carlos Castaneda's The Teachings of Don Juan: A Yaqui Way of Knowledge. We learned how to identify with space that has no mass. It was like touching the mystery. Chuck chose a small group of us and formed the Magic Mountain Mime Troupe. We practiced in the woods and engaged in unseen spatial relationships. I learned how to feel subtle vibrations and spent days communicating non-verbally. One day I ate thirteen mushrooms, and I don't think I ever came down from that.

Excelling at FSU, I was able to get into an independent program to study theater abroad. I wrote my own curriculum to take me to London. I was bubbling over to think I'd be hopping my first silver bird, whizzing across the ocean at incredible speeds to a new country.

A tizzy of activity swirled around me as I prepared for the journey. Practicing my British wenching accent in a cockney style had my college buddies belly-laughing at my theatrical antics. There was only one obstacle to overcome. Unlike all my friends, I didn't have a birth certificate. To get a passport, I needed proof of my birth. I was determined to get that piece of paper.

Finagling a Passport

When summer arrived, I drove back to my parents and told them about my plans. I asked for my birth certificate so I could get a passport. They were totally against me traveling out of the country. I dropped the subject, played the good daughter, and worked on a scheme.

I discovered I'd be able to get my birth certificate if I had a copy of both of my parents. I told Mom and Dad I was researching our family to build a family tree. They were cooperative with sharing information about their own heritage. After I made a three-generation family tree, I asked for a copy of their birth certificates. What I didn't tell them was I needed those copies to get a passport. Bingo.

I wove through the haze of busy streets still strewn with debris from the hurricane that had skirted past us. After circling downtown, I spotted a place to park my VW bug. The sky opened up in a drenching downpour as I jumped out. Tucking my folder under my bright blue raincoat, I pulled up my hood and dashed down the street, sloshing my way to the enormous doors of the Miami courthouse. The lobby was packed with Cubans, and I sidestepped my way through to the elevator and squeezed in as the door closed. My folder was safe and dry, clasped to my pounding chest.

When it was my turn to speak to a county official, I plopped down my folder and announced that I needed a birth certificate to get a passport. The woman said, "I need to see a photo ID and your social security card." I didn't have a social security card either, which made my request even more challenging. Opening my folder, I pulled out copies of my parents' birth certificates, my driver's license, college records, and a letter of acceptance into Florida State University's study-abroad program.

The woman looked me in the eye for the first time, saying my papers were sufficient. Unexpected tears slid down my already wet cheeks as she told me to have a seat while she searched for records.

What seemed like hours went by until she reappeared and motioned me over. I was 22 when I first got a copy of my birth certificate. Giving her a big smile, I paid my bill and quickly returned to my car to look it over in private.

The certificate listed the hospital I was born in. The "informant" listed was my dad, and my mom's maiden name was misspelled. I knew it wasn't my real one. How can a government agency lie about who gave birth to me? Gasping to catch my breath, I watched my car windows fog up, leaving me in a hidden bubble. At least I had a birth certificate, albeit fake, and I could get a passport.

My research revealed the hospital code listed did not match the hospital. I called around, trying to find the Edgewater Hospital to discover my birth records. Disconnected phone numbers and dead ends provided no leads except an address. I drove to the location, and there was no indication that a hospital had ever been there, nor did anyone I talked to in the area know anything about it.

Searching further at the Miami library, I discovered the hospital had burned down, along with all the records. Ultimately, having a birth certificate in hand spewed even more mysteries.

My parents never talked about it. I did ask a few more times if I had another mother. After my drinking episode my mother jokingly said that if I did have one, she must have been a drunk and was dead. They still denied I was adopted, but in my gut I knew it. With no names to go by, I spun my wheels looking through newspaper articles. How was it that someone was able to steal my identity, rob my heritage and keep me from knowing the truth? Of what use was the deception behind all of this, and to whom? Who in this world could I truly trust? My sense of betrayal led me to believe I could only trust myself. That became my modus vivendi. But I was soon on my way to London, and my investigation fell by the wayside for a while.

3

THE WISH

In London, I got to study at Berman's Costume House, the Young Vic Theater, and assist Martin Esslin at the BBC. On holiday break, a few friends and I pooled funds and bought an old bright purple International Harvester truck to travel around in. Our excitement waned after we ran it without oil. We abandoned it on a back road near Paris and split up, thinking it'd be easier to hitchhike that way. The plan was to meet up in a small fishing village called Torremolinos on the coast of Spain and go to Africa. This was way before cell phones, and looking back on that time, it's hard to believe I set out alone with no way to contact my friends. After a few harrowing experiences on the road, I made it to the coast, but I was the only one. I hung around a few more days on the black beaches, which turned out to be touristy and expensive, then headed to the tip of Spain and caught a boat to Africa.

Stolen Passport

Passing by the Rock of Gibraltar, I felt uneasy about traveling alone, but it was too late to turn back. I disembarked in Tangiers, Morocco. It seemed like every guy's name was

Abdul, and they wanted to sell me hashish. They tried to convince me to stuff it in a belt or the soles of my shoes to go unnoticed. I kept moving on and slipped into what I thought was a safe restaurant. They obliged me by cooking up some couscous with my bottled water and brought out an array of cheeses. Then the owner came to my table with a hookah and offered me hashish for dessert. Everywhere I went, the custom was to offer a foreigner hashish.

I got out of the city and train-hopped to Fez for a day and then onto Maknesh. The smaller towns had fewer hawkers, fewer horns, and more bicycle riders with friendly faces. From there, I visited the famed Casablanca. I found a hotel and checked in for a few days. On the rooftop at sunset, I took in a striking view of Casablanca. A dappled quilt of blues, whites, and terra cotta buildings spread out before me. As my eyes followed the patchwork of colors, it merged into the ocean blues of the vast Atlantic. The cool breeze and relative quiet were a reprieve from my hectic traveling. I spent the next day journaling under a large white umbrella with my feet buried in the sand at the water's edge.

All was well until I ventured south and rented an open-windowed hut for a night. While I was sleeping, someone stole my backpack and passport. I was clueless as to what to do. I had a bit of money in my pocket and the clothes on my back. Some foreigners I met told me to go to the American Embassy in Marrakesh, and I'd get help there.

I hopped a train to Marrakesh, then walked on foot towards the embassy. I came across a dozen hippies sitting under the only tree in sight. They had makeshift shade cloths tied off from the tree and a little camp stove boiling up coffee. I approached, asking where the embassy was, and they welcomed me to join them. We exchanged stories, and I felt more comfortable knowing I wasn't alone in having a passport stolen. Some of them had been waiting for weeks to get theirs. They informed me the embassy was further away, and they were packing up to head back there. The embassy had closed for some Moroccan Independence holiday. It was supposed to have reopened, but they said it was impossible to figure out its hours. From rumors, they surmised it was only open in the mornings on certain days, and each day seemed to have a different closing time. Disorganized as it was, I was glad to be with comrades that knew more than I did.

I did get help at the embassy to contact the USA to get money wired. Getting a passport replacement was another ordeal. With no identification, I had to undergo various security checks, which took days to get approved. With school break almost over, I then high-tailed it back to London. No shots were needed to get out of England or into France, Spain, or Africa, but I had to get a bunch to get back into London. The sight of needles knocked me off my feet, and all the shots messed me up for a year after that. Suffice it to say, I ended up having to return to my parent's home to recuperate.

Return Home

My parents were relieved I was alive but appalled I had traipsed off to Africa. I didn't tell them much about my adventures, which would only worsen matters. They were worried about my state of being, and I was worried about hurting them. Of course, they reminded me they'd told me not to leave the USA in the first place.

I wasn't much help on the home front. Mom was getting weaker and diagnosed with breast cancer. She went back and forth between doctor's appointments and the hospital. The house smelled like an infirmary, and my fainting spells began again. I was useless in giving the support Mom needed.

My parents wanted me to finish college in Tallahassee, so I returned to FSU. Psilocybin helped center me again and get back on track. Still looking for answers to life's mysteries, I switched my major from theater to religion. My idea was to focus on overlapping stories and myths from different religions and try to make sense of it all.

Most religious texts are various versions of the same theme. However, the roots of humanity's existence all seem too much like fairy tales. I switched majors again, this time to philosophy. The final paper I wrote was about my own philosophy of religion. My basic premise was that the universe is like a bagel. In the center is unlimited potential, and everything surrounding that is what we as creators manifest. The bagel's edges expand as our imagination and consciousness embrace our ability to create. I called it "The Bagel Philosophy." My professor, Dr. Ice, was not amused. But it's still what I believe to this day.

I decided everything that happens is just a drama, and we're all playing our parts in the theater of life. Wasn't I simply passing through another stage in the big divine show? In my last year, I switched majors back to Theater Arts and dabbled in costuming, directing, acting, and music. Then I discovered Mom's breast cancer had gotten worse, and she was undergoing intense chemotherapy. I needed to go home.

Ann and I were still in contact and I told her the bad news. She contacted her mentor, Dr. Roberta Baker, the head costumer at the University of Miami's Ring Theater. Ann recommended me as an intern for a scholarship so I could work on a Master of Arts degree and be closer to home. It was the #1 party school in the nation, and I thought it might lighten the intensity at home.

Wenching for Bucks

I received the scholarship and wound up specializing in costuming. My good friend Jodee, who'd also been at FSU with me, enrolled too. Wanting to make some extra bucks, we auditioned for a job as singing-dancing waitresses at a restaurant called 1520 AD in Miami Beach. We arrived costumed as wenches and both cinched a job. Soon our bloomers were stuffed with dough.

Jodee's mom had a nationally known dance and costume company and was a head honcho in the Florida dance community. She told us a big ball was coming up and that they'd hired various performers for the event. We decided it'd be fun to disguise ourselves and crash the party.

Posing as roaming performers, we arrived decked out in wigs and makeup. We cashed in by going up to blokes saying, "It's a dollar a dance, a fiver for a kiss, and twenty for a roll in the hay." When we left, our pockets and bosoms bulged with cash.

Later, we heard two performers at the ball were in high demand, but no one knew who they were. We confessed it was us and took time off from school and our server jobs to do some wenching for clients. We were so busy that we soon began teaching others how to wench to meet the demand.

Cancer, Seizures, and Requests

On the home front things were getting worse. Mom was seriously struggling with her cancer. She went through chemo, lost her hair, and then her breasts. She still managed to dress up and had an array of wigs.

Because of my weird fainting spells happening at the most inappropriate times, they tried to keep me away from her.

The Edgar Cayce remedies I used worked well, but living in a 24/7 environment of hospital smells of antiseptics and disinfectants nauseated me. I kept antispasmodic tincture and smelling salts on me, and most of the time I could prevent fainting or at least get down on the ground so I didn't crash.

A convulsive daughter wasn't needed around when Mom was battling cancer. She hung in there and encouraged me to finish my Master of Arts at her alma mater. Then she wanted me to find a nice man, get married, and settle down while she was still alive. That wish had my eyes rolling.

In my last semester at the University of Miami, I landed a job as the costumer for the world premiere of a show called Equus at the Coconut Grove Playhouse. It was a dream job and Mom was so proud of me. During that time, I became close friends with Jay, the show's technical director. Mom liked him and reminded me of her dying wish to see me get married.

Unlikely Union

When I told Jay of Mom's wish, he said, "Let's do it!" He was serious, but the thought of marriage terrified me. We had dinner together and talked more about the situation. His parents had been onto him about getting married too. The more we talked, the better it sounded. I told him to give me a few days to think it through.

The next day I stirred up my creative juices. Why not stage a wedding? It could be fun. Of course, I'd want prenuptial agreements drawn up in case something didn't work out. I researched and discovered that turning a marriage decree over to governmental authorities wasn't mandatory. My only trepidation was the feeling that I'd be indebted to him. I came up with an idea to make it work. I'd offer to do whatever he wanted for the first three years.

When I laid out my plan to Jay, he was all for it. He upped the ante by saying that he'd do whatever I wanted to do for the three years after that. We were on!

A few nights later, Jay proposed to me backstage. Someone turned a red spotlight on us as he presented me with a sparkling diamond engagement ring. The theater crew gathered around raising a toast to us, and the fun began. We set a date for the end of summer and announced the wedding plans.

Historic Plymouth Congregational Church was a magical sanctuary a few blocks from the playhouse and the perfect place to stage our union. I found an antique ivory wedding dress that Mom loved. The reception dinner would be on Key Biscayne, where I spent a lot of time with my mom as a kid. Excitement filled the air, and Mom's eyes twinkled in delight.

Making my own wedding cake was somewhat disastrous but edible, at least. A giant poster covering my bedroom door read, "Always take on more than you can handle or you'll never do all that you can do." Remembering that helped me get through the wedding preparations. When the big day finally came, I thought I'd have to toothpick my eyes open. Jodee was my maid of honor and supported me through all of this. She found me asleep and half-crocked on champagne when she got to the church. Helping me dress, she managed to get the 25 or more tiny buttons on the back of my gown closed while trying to calm my jitters. It all seemed too real!

It was time to show myself. Dad was there waiting to walk me down the aisle as the organ played "Here Comes the Bride." Seeing my nervousness, Dad gently squeezed my hand as the march began, and he quietly sang into my ear.

Instead of hearing "Love now triumphant forever unites," he sang a song he'd playfully sung to me many times in my childhood to get me to laugh. "Oh, they chew tobacco thin in Mobile, in Mobile. Oh, they chew tobacco thin and it runs right down their chin. Oh, they chew tobacco thin in Mobile." I grinned ear to ear as we made our entrance down the aisle.

The wedding was a success. I'd never seen Mom so blissed out. Even my Aunt Lilly, who called to tell me she'd never stepped into a church before in her life and wasn't about to now, showed up from Baltimore and gave her blessings.

I goofed up serving shellfish at the reception. That was a huge mistake for the Jewish part of the family. A few friends came to the rescue, showing up with assorted deli platters. They escorted the Jewish constituency to a spread of Rabbi-blessed wines, pastrami, borscht, and kugel, on the far side of the room away from the forbidden non-kosher foods. By the time they toasted with champagne and downed some schnapps and Manischewitz, they didn't seem to notice my blunder and were thoroughly enjoying themselves.

After the cake ritual and dance, we escaped to our hideout. We'd reserved the top suite of the Mutiny Hotel close by. Gifts were sent over, and we laughed for hours as we shamelessly opened our booty while consuming some excellent South Florida sacrament. We totally cracked up when opening a fourth set of grapefruit spoons. One set was engraved with a B, obviously from his part of the family. We decided the B stood for booty since I'd kept my last name.

We awoke late, surrounded by piles of wrapping paper and cards. I panicked when realizing we hadn't kept the cards with the gifts and had no idea who had sent what. I made a list of the gifts and shuffled all the cards together, thinking we'd figure it out on our honeymoon. We were going sailing!

Our escape bags were ready on our 40' Alden Cutter, docked across the street at Monty Trainer's marina. For our first three years, Jay had chosen for us to live on a sailboat, which sounded adventurous enough to me.

Our parents thought they'd soon be grandparents … as we sailed off into the sunset with our secret.

Howdy Doody

After extensive sailing, we returned and made our home base docked in Coconut Grove. I worked on television commercials and independent films for a while. Then I landed a job as the costume designer for the remake of NBC's Howdy Doody Show, featuring most of the original cast. We all had to bust it to keep up with the demands of the producers. There was a show every weekday, and we only got the script five days ahead of time. We worked every day from early in the morning till way after sunset. It was a fun job, but it raised some issues for me.

Kids in the "peanut gallery" and millions of children fixated on their TVs believed that Howdy's sister, Heidi, was adopted. No one explained who Howdy or Heidi's parents were. It was thought that Howdy adopted his sister. Yes, they were puppets, but despite that, the message made light of adoption. It seemed that it didn't matter where they came from. As an adoptee, we're often told the rhetoric that we were adopted into a good family and shouldn't care about our past. But we do, and it shouldn't be a secret.

After immersing myself in Doodyville for over 100 episodes, I was ready for a change of pace. I designed another children's show and a few operas for the Greater Miami Opera. Then I costumed a few films and continued working as a freelance stylist for commercials.

After a few years of living on a sailboat together, Jay and I needed more elbow room. We bought a stunning historic Spanish-style home in Coral Gables. But even with the spaciousness of our grand abode, our paths began to diverge. At the end of our three-year agreement, we parted ways.

I rented a funky old house on Key Biscayne and took on even more jobs. I reveled in my work. Being busy was my excuse to not let on to Mom that Jay and I were history.

There was always some new challenge to conquer. My busy life left no time to search for my roots. In a way, it was great not to have family responsibilities or to answer to anyone. There was no tethering to hold me down. I was free … but I was alone.

4

IDENTITY THEFT

I began a serious search for my bio parents after my adoptive parents passed away. Mom went first, on Mother's Day, after struggling for years with complications from her breast cancer. Dad passed on later from a heart attack after sending out humorous invitations for his centenarian birthday celebration. He said it's never too early to plan a party, even if he wouldn't be around.

Losing my parents re-triggered my deep wound of abandonment. The loss and grief only strengthened my skepticism about intimacy. I'd chosen not to have children for various reasons, and besides my brother, Lee, whom I rarely saw, I was alone in the world.

I still didn't know for sure that I was adopted, but there was nothing to stop me from searching now. Maybe I'd find a clue to unveil decades of secrets in Dad's closely guarded file cabinets. I looked through his closet and office and found multiple keys. A few fit his desk drawers, and I rummaged through papers which all seemed recent. Next, I explored the garage where six large metal file cabinets were. I got them open, but after pilfering through hundreds of files, I came up empty-handed. A small ancient cabinet about half the size of the others was tucked in behind them. The last and tiniest key popped it open, exploding musty air into my jaw-dropped mouth. There it was, a blue folder with the label: Final Decree of Adoption.

I slid it up and saw my brother's name. Even though Lee said he never wanted to know anything, I was anxious to tell him. It baffled me that anyone wouldn't be curious about their origins. Tucking it back in, I kept digging through the tightly stuffed files. In the back was another blue folder, pushed halfway down.

I gently tugged the folder up enough to see my name. Frozen in time, it was all I could do to touch it. My monkey mind jumped into doubt. Was it the right time to do this? Did I even want to know? Maybe this was a mistake. After all, I'd had a good life, and my parents wouldn't appreciate my prying. Could they peer down on me now, breaking into their private records?

A mixture of shame, fear, anxiety, and dizziness thwarted my deep desire to know the truth. I was sweating in the heat of the garage and shivering at the same time. This was no time to faint. My head spun with what-ifs. Calling in for support from the universe, a voice said, "Breathe, just keep breathing and you'll be all right." Maybe it was my own voice, but whatever it was, it worked.

The blue-backed legal-size file was shaking between my fingers. No matter what I'd find, I had to know. Pulling it out, I hugged it to my chest and sat on the cabinet with it on my lap. Closing my eyes, I asked for strength and support for whatever I'd discover and invoked help from the Almighty with all my heart and soul. Gripping the folder, my long fingers trembled, rumpling it. I quickly smoothed the old papers, running my hand over them numerous times.

The decree was indeed of my adoption. The first page referred to me as Infant Hanson. Having a name to go by was a goldmine, or at least that's what I thought at the time. Hanson, oh my God, that's a Dutch name. My parents must have known I was a Hanson when giving me wooden clogs as a child. Dad's brother, Uncle Melvin, must have also been in on the secret because he brought me gifts from his frequent European travels that always included Dutch chocolates and blue and white pottery trinkets. My blonde hair, blue eyes, and love for cheese and chocolates were all very Dutchy.

Pilfering through the rest of Dad's papers, I uncovered his letter to Florida Vital Statistics dated April 1967, requesting my birth certificate and social security number. I was already in high school by that time. I didn't exist in the system, as Dad's letter stated that Dade County had no record of me.

Excavating further, I found a receipt of payment to an attorney for my adoption. It never occurred to me that I was paid for. My imagination spun all over the place, and when it settled, I decided I must be a black-market baby. My identity was stolen, and I was bought!

Alien Blood

I got my first electronic desktop brain and started mining for answers. I discovered there had been an illegitimate adoption ring in Miami in the fifties. A woman doctor named Cole had delivered over 1,000 babies and sold them! She falsified birth certificates and turned over infants without any actual legal papers. How did she get away with that? She secretly provided housing for pregnant women who were primarily unwed or poor. Cole was buried in 1981 under a shroud of deception. To this day, many adoptees searching for their biological roots are unaware of this clandestine operation, and many have already passed away without ever knowing the truth.

This is a serious issue when you realize adoption is a multi-billion dollar enterprise. In 2022, the industry made over a whopping 21 billion. It's a profiteering business with much human trafficking that must be de-commodified. Adoptees are the vulnerable sitting duck in the equation, but their protection and support need the most attention.

I furiously explored the internet as it exploded open Pandora's box. Cole's clinic was a few miles from Edgewater Hospital, where I was supposedly born. My birth certificate hospital code didn't match up with Edgewater's code. This made it even more complicated. So far, I really didn't know where I was born. Online forums about the Edgewater Hospital proved to be a gold mine. An unusual number of adoptees searching for their families were born there in the 1950s.

I posted some information about my search that evoked a flurry of responses. Like me, other adoptees heard the hospital burned down with all the records. Some thought it was a cover-up for a black-market baby racket. The scam was selling babies without going through the strict adoption procedures. Doesn't that sound a bit like slavery?

Conspiracy theories were running amuck. On another forum called "Above Secret," I found something even freakier. Copious amounts of adoptees posted about having O-negative blood. Some believed they were experimental kryptonite test-tube babies put up for adoption and kept under surveillance. Most of them also had blond hair and blue eyes. What if I were like them?

I got a blood test kit, closed my eyes, pricked my finger, and discovered I had O-negative blood! This blood has no Rhesus factor or A or B antibodies. A lot of these adoptees claimed they were from non-human origins. Some thought their ancestors bred with extraterrestrials. That could explain why I never fit in. I remembered the biblical texts that said the angels came and mated with the pretty women. A few other adoptees said they were descendants of the Hyperboreans, a Greek mythical race of giants with blond hair and blue eyes. I wondered if the Dutch were from this race.

Having access to computer data created one befuddlement after another. I soon filled dozens of floppy disks with my research. Posting messages on a few O-negative sites, I asked if adoptees with O-negative blood were born under mysterious circumstances. The answer was yes. Interestingly, most of them also involved Masonic connections.

I found no clear information on where this blood type came from. Why were there so many adoptees with mysterious births that had O-negative blood? Probing further into the alien connection, it turned out that over one-third of reported abductees have O-negative blood! Is it because O-negatives have wild imaginations? Mine was undoubtedly running rampant.

O-negative people can't take blood from any other blood type, yet they can give theirs to anyone. A pregnant O-negative woman must take drugs to have a baby if her partner has a different blood type. Otherwise, the baby's red blood cells can be attacked, causing a miscarriage. That's weird. Interestingly, the word "alien" comes from the Latin alienus, meaning "belonging to another." Since adoption created the situation where I belonged to another, and I had found the receipt to prove it, and my blood type was of unknown origin, I decided that made me a double alien.

Like me, many O-negative adoptees were healthy and had high energy levels and low blood pressure. Networking with them, I discovered that psychic and paranormal experiences were more common in our blood group. I'd certainly had my share of mystical episodes and intense visions that impelled me to act upon them.

My mind collided with worldly logic as I tried to grasp what it all meant. What about some of the religious texts I'd studied that referred to flying machines? There were too many references to dismiss. And what was the Holy Grail? Was it the cup used to collect Jesus's blood at the crucifixion? Was his blood O-negative? What about the Biblical mention of the blessed seed of the children of Israel? Why were they warned not to marry outside their tribe? And what about the circumcision of baby boys mandated in the Torah? Why in Genesis does it say that Jewish males must be circumcised as an everlasting covenant in their flesh, and if they don't, they'll be cut off from the tribe? Was it to guard their DNA? But where did original humans come from? If Adam and Eve were the only humans, where did their sons get wives? Did anyone know where any of us came from?

Further down the rabbit hole, I found that all living beings, animals included, can naturally breed with any other individuals of their species, except for those with O-negative blood. Everything I learned only led to more questions. Why is blood the second most used word in biblical texts? What do the Bible and other ancient cultures mean by "the blood of God"? The more questions I sought answers for, the more complex it became.

It left me thinking I was some kind of experimental hybrid from an alien abduction or the result of fornication by some fallen angel. Or maybe they were one and the same. This new knowledge loaded with conspiracy theories drove me bonkers. I had to step back and remind myself I was the sanest person I knew. That in itself was scary.

I had to find out who or what birthed me.

5

NON-IDENTIFYING INFORMATION

I enrolled in numerous groups that were clearinghouses for adoptees and birth parents. Most of the registries and associations I signed up for involved snail-mailing applications with payment and then waiting for a lucky day when someone might contact me. Three decades later, I still was not one of the fortunate ones that got a response. It's much easier in the 21st century to find one's bio-family than in the 70s. Today there are hundreds of databases to search from, plus inexpensive DNA testing.

I discovered I could file with the state for "non-identifying information" about my birth. I forged through the roadblocks, jumped through all the hoops, and filed. Then I petitioned the state of Florida to recognize that a human being has more rights than a mattress. After all, a mattress has a tag that says, "Do not remove under penalty of law," and all that tag says is where it's made and what it's made from. Didn't I have at least the rights of a mattress? The official answer was "No." However, I eventually received the non-identifying info.

The document was disappointing, but I got a few hints to narrow my search. It reported, "Your mother was from the largest far western coastal state. She was 5'5", 125 pounds, had blonde hair and blue eyes, and loved to dance." Imagine trying to find someone in California matching that description. It also said that her birthday was about a week after mine and that she was 26. She had never been married, and I was her first child. My birth father was 29, born circa 1921, he was 6'2" and weighed 200 pounds. He was an only child in a highly political family from a major Midwestern urban center. It stated he knew of my birth and felt adoption was the best plan.

At least I learned that he knew about me. My mind branded him as a creep. How could he get someone pregnant and walk away? How callous and inhumane he must have been. Why would I ever want to know this cold and heartless person? The warrior in me came forward and polished my armor, guarding me against men. I bet my mother was forced to give me up because my father wouldn't support her, and he didn't want me.

I narrowed my search to look for a woman named Hanson in California, born the last week of June in the mid-1920s. This was even more challenging since I didn't know when I was born. I fiercely flung myself down one hole after another, digging up anything that might help me. In the end, not one birth certificate or social security record matched up.

Reluctantly, I then checked for Hanson men born between 1920-1922. Scouring through adoption records in every midwestern state left me empty-handed. Political and military records in the Midwest and California also proved to be useless. Then I repeated the entire process using variations of the name Hanson. After all, my adoptive mother's name was misspelled on my birth certificate. How could authorities be so careless in recording details on such vital records? Didn't they know how important it was? The warrioress in me was fatigued from the continual battle in the search for truth. It wasn't fair that I spent years on the front line and had nothing to show for it.

The theft and erasure of anyone's identity is a crime. I needed professional help in more ways than one. What I most wanted now was a sleuthy Sherlock Holmes in a black-and-white checkered coat with a magnifying glass in his pocket. Yes, with a bloodhound to track down my birth father. But could I trust anyone else to help me? I really didn't have a choice.

Detectives

I rooted around for days, reading the references of various detectives, and narrowed it down to five. I wrote down their names and dowsed them with a pendulum that resembles a plumb bob. Mine was a carnelian stone carved into a spinning top hanging from a gold chain. I programmed it to give me a yes-or-no answer to questions. I held it still above a name, and it circled to the left; that was a no. The next one swung to the right, and that was a yes. I got one more yes out of the five, and the two yeses were both men. Go figure!

I flipped a coin and chose one. I sent him a retainer and a summary of what I'd done and waited. Days went by with no word. When I got ahold of him, he told me things already in my summary. I let him go and went on to my second detective. I told him to thoroughly review my summary before hiring him to ensure he had other avenues to pursue. Later that day, he assured me he had contacts on the inside that no one else had. He was sure he could help me. I hired him and waited.

Within a week, he gave me a Hanson's first, middle, and last name, along with her birthday of June 26, 1923. He also gave me an address in Miami, where she'd been staying at the time of my birth. I had already searched all the Hansons in California and didn't find this. That name wasn't there when I looked through all the records I'd kept. I then did a new search and found no one by that name. It seemed clear to me he was fabricating this. I told the detective there was no record of this person, and he told me he had been able to get into my sealed records. Since I couldn't verify what he told me, I figured I'd gotten taken again.

I drove to the Miami address he gave me, and there had never been a house there. I wanted to put a bloodhound on both of these tacky gumshoe spies.

Inner Community

How would I find her after all the work I'd done with no promising results? By this time, my friends were telling me she might be dead. Do not ever tell an adoptee something like that! If you're not adopted, you will never understand the pain that statement can conjure.

My inner community characters, as I call the various actors inside my head, were fighting. One assured me I'd find my birth mother, another said, "Don't be stupid! You'll never find her." Another said, "Just put it aside for a while and get out of your funk." Another prompted me to cry and get through the grief about it. Yet another said, "You know, you need professional help." Well, she was the voice that made the most sense to me at that moment.

I'd never had counseling but found myself searching for someone specializing in adoptees. I found an adoptee retreat was happening soon in the Virgin Islands. Joe Soll, the author of Adoption Healing, A Path to Recovery, was the event's facilitator. It sounded right up my alley. He was the only certified social worker I found whose work focused on adoptees. Without further investigation, I booked the retreat and a flight.

Finding My Tribe

Seven of us flew to St. Croix, and this was the first time any of us had connected with other adoptees. Being around those who could understand my plight opened the floodgates. We exposed ourselves in raw vulnerability, leading to grieving and some serious group hugs.

I learned so much about myself in that three-day retreat. The information we received helped us identify ourselves. We learned about the primal wound when an infant is removed from a mother's energies at birth. The repercussions of this can last a lifetime, especially if the adoptee doesn't understand that their issues are related to that trauma.

Like me, adoptees can be high achievers that strive for attention. That may have been what made me such a mover and shaker. Three of us at the retreat fell into that category. Every one of us shared we had difficulty bonding with others as well as having trust issues. Some adoptees go into the pitiful "I'm not loved" mode. Others go into the independent, "I don't need anyone's help" mode. I knew which one I was, without a doubt.

I read his latest book in our off time and did all the prompts and exercises. Joe totally believes that lies only deepen the wound. He says it's much healthier to deal with the truth.

Infants don't understand the loss and cannot rationally process grief, but it's there and needs to be addressed early in life.

Adoptee issues can be triggered at any moment in life. Identity, intimate relationships, shame, abandonment, loss, grief, secrecy, commitment, and control are some of the complex issues that affect adoptees throughout their lives. It's not only adoptees who are traumatized. All triad members suffer, the adoptees, birth parents, and adoptive parents. Issues of infertility, having a baby out of wedlock, family pressure, secrets, shame, blame, and a myriad of other circumstances lace the situation with suffering. Regardless of the situation, these issues must not be swept under the rug. Children have the right to know the truth, the right to understand their heritage, the right to their biological medical information, and not to be lied to. Sealed records, fabrications, and lies lead to adversity.

Most adoptee issues are buried in everyday life. The biggest one is typically trust. Separation destroys a baby's embryonic sense of trust. The adoptive parents can try to patch up the wound, but many aren't aware of it or have the skills to address it. The separation wound remains no matter how caring the adoptee's parents are. Blood bonds stay with us all, whether we're conscious of it or not.

In my case, I masked awareness of the idiosyncrasies caused by being relinquished for four decades of my life. Coping mechanisms developed throughout my youth with no understanding of what was happening. I became a confronting, controlling warrioress, unable to commit to relationships. I didn't know then that every relationship I got into was processed through my infant lens of relinquishment. Only now do I understand I had an insecure attachment bond.

On the positive side, I developed a deep desire for esoteric knowledge. I wanted to know what was hidden. That was easier than relating to people. Like me, many adoptees hold back their feelings because they feel in debt to their adoptive parents. They should be grateful they're alive, right? That in itself puts the adoptee in a state of debt. I never wanted to be in debt to anyone, especially my parents. They had done so much for me already. I needed to prove I could care for things and stand up independently. This gave me a boost to be successful in my business enterprises. I never wanted to work for anyone else. In retrospect, I think it was because of my need to be in control and not under anyone's thumb.

The late adoption scholar and activist Reverend Keith C. Griffith once said, "Adoption Loss is the only trauma in the world where the victims are expected by the whole of society to be grateful."

I was ultimately fortunate to value the gifts of my unusual life. I became a strong woman, but the consequences of my hidden coping mechanisms sorely hampered my relationships and social skills. Being a victim of adoption can give one the impetus to develop a strong character, but I think one's DNA plays an integral role in whether that happens. Often, adoptees feel less than whole and that something is wrong with them. It's the adoption system itself that something is wrong with. Change needs to happen, and unfortunately, it's the adoptees who are having to fight to make those changes.

I felt like I'd met my tribe at the retreat. We were all on an emotional roller coaster jarring us out of our comfort zones. The upheaval unveiled deep unconscious wounds that had scabbed over but had never healed. My scars remained, but at least I knew what was happening when they itched.

I came away with new friends and insights about my physiological limitations and strengths. Learning how to balance what I learned emotionally, physically, mentally, and spiritually would be ongoing. The investigation into knowing who we are is a demanding task, but that's what's needed to develop emotional intelligence. I had a good start because I left with a vital gift: compassion for myself. With that, I was able to have more compassion for my inner community, and we all needed to step back and incorporate these new insights. As Socrates said, "An unexamined life is not worth living."

6

REVOLVER PERSUASION

The huge change after the adoptee immersion was my inner community quit arguing. That was an enormous blessing as I had a variety of projects to stay on top of that were challenging to balance with my search. Did I want to spend my entire life looking for a stranger when the world was going crazy, and the environment was the utmost important issue on the planet? Did it really matter if I found her? I talked myself into believing that it wasn't that important. I set the wild goose chase down again and went on about my life.

Unexpectedly, a sweet, adorable, purse-size mutt came into my life. A soft, creamy ball of fur, a Lhasa Aspö with peekaboo eyes. She reminded me of the Jewish soup balls I'd eaten often in my youth. I wasn't going to have children, so to honor my Dad's Jewish heritage, I named her Matzaball. I adopted her, and we became inseparable. Matzaball gave me a glimpse of unconditional love.

I graduated from the University of Miami with a Master of Arts, specializing in costume design. Jumping back into the work game, I was fortunate to land famous clients in the U.S. and England. My cockney-wenching accent was a hit with the British crews, and I caught on quickly to their rhyming slang. They'd call and hire me to "muck around," as they say. I was a bit of an entertainer for them, and they appreciated my costume and stylist work. I freelanced for eight years, working on television commercials and films, living in New York, Miami, and Los Angeles.

Since money wasn't a problem, I considered adopting kids by mail. It wasn't the typical adoption process; I'd just provide them food, school supplies, clothes, and education. I figured it wouldn't be time-consuming, and I'd be doing something positive. So many children have no family, home, or basic necessities, and I was in a position to do something about it. I didn't need to clone myself by having children. My sock monkey and Matzaball seemed to be enough. Where might I tell my kids they came from anyway? It also didn't make sense to me with our planet's condition. So, I adopted a few mail-order kids from Guatemala and supported them until they were 18. With kids and a dog, I figured I was set.

It wasn't until 1980 that I decided to quit the film industry and give up working for big corporations. How did that contribute to making our planet better for future generations? What was I doing with my life besides having fun and making bucks?

I'd had a great ride in the industry but had refused to join the union. This is a most sought-after membership, but I applied and was rejected early on. Fortunately, Florida was a right-to-work state. I was good at what I did and was hired anyway. After a while, I made more money than some union members, which didn't go over well. There were a few strikes on sets I was on because of it. They said I had to join the union, but I didn't see how it benefited me. By this time, I understood that some union members got in not because of skill but because they were family, lovers, or something else.

I'd become friends with some producers and directors who appreciated my work. It aggravated them when a strike happened on their shooting schedule. To my surprise, they told me they'd support me if I wanted to fight the union. That seemed like a big hassle, but I kept it in mind. It wasn't long before I was seriously harassed. I was in my Winnebago getting costumes ready for a shoot when a tall, heavy-set man I'd never seen before came in. He told me I needed to slow down on the set, or there'd be trouble. I retorted I was hired because I got a good job done in a timely manner and … while I babbled, he slid up his shirt and pulled out a 45 revolver.

Without thinking, I let out a deafening "Don't shoot!" Matzaball yelped, and a woman came to the door to see what the commotion was about. He walked out in a huff telling the woman everything was fine and to go about her business. Grabbing Matzaball, I hugged her as tight as I could. I didn't want to cause a scene on the set, so I kept it to myself until the shoot ended. Afterward, I talked to the producer and director who'd offered to help me, and they were on board with a plan. The next day, I called the National Relations Labor Board and filed suit against the union for harassment in a right-to-work state. They took my case on.

When the trial date came, my opponents had no idea what was in my back pocket. They fabricated stories with no proof. Then my witnesses came in and blew them away with plenty of documentation of harassment and their loss of income because of the strikes. They ruled the case in my favor and shut the union down in Florida, which was a first. It wasn't a prolonged shutdown, but even a day was too much for them, much less a month.

I kept working for companies not dominated by the union. About a week after the trial, I was on a Toyota commercial. I mentioned to the art director that I was dreaming about a Celica GT sports coupe with a four-way sound system, coffee warmer, blow dryer, tinted windows, and teak roof rack. Much to my surprise, he said he could handle that, and I could get it wholesale. When the car arrived in California, I flew out and drove my new ride cross-country back home.

A few days later, the producer of another commercial I was working on asked about renting a sailboat to go out in Biscayne Bay. After my three years with Jay had ended, I got into a relationship with Robin, a dynamic, playful physical therapist. Robin was also a sailor and had a perfect boat for a group cruise. Robin and I had remained good friends after we ended our infatuation. He was interested in marriage and babies, and even though he was a hunkaluv, that wasn't on my radar. I called him and we arranged a sunset sail for the film crew.

It was the full moon of August in 1980. Pushing off from the dock at twilight, the sun set behind us as the moon peeked up over the horizon. Hoisting the sails, the warm breeze gently waltzed us back and forth across the beam of moonlight, luring us toward her luminous presence. It was one of those perfect nights. The spectacular ambiance kept us all in silent awe for hours.

When we returned to the dock in Coconut Grove, we were stunned out of our serene state. My new dream car was gone. It only took a few minutes to surmise it was related to the lawsuit. I called the police as Robin wrapped his arm around me, asking what he could do. Gasping for breath, I said,

"Draw me a map. I know you have 500 acres somewhere in North Carolina."

I'd never thought about not having a home base in Miami, and it surprised me I'd even consider it. A friend from childhood had recently visited me from Tennessee and wanted me to come up to the mountains. Maybe I needed a sabbatical from all the drama and go up there and then to Robin's land. Why not take a month off?

My dream car had vanished. Somehow, the records at the DMV had disappeared, and I didn't know my license number. The car was full of things I needed for a shoot the next day. Included in the booty were state trooper uniforms, items to return from the previous shoot, and contents from my safe deposit box, which I had picked up that afternoon. The police found some items the next day in a nearby park with a bunch of things I could do without strewn around the area, but that was it.

When Robin gave me the map, I considered heading out of dodge. Then a few days later, my home was broken into. The only possessions obviously missing were my files from the court case. Next, my brother reported my nephew's clothes went missing at his house. That was the determining factor. I let go of just about everything and booked a ticket to Tennessee.

Catapulted

I dressed Matzaball in a bright blue T-shirt and bandana she'd gotten at a film shoot and took off on an adventure. When I stepped off the plane, the weight of years working in the film industry slid off my back. The lush mountains became a nurturing haven for me. It didn't take long to decide to sell my home in Miami. I was ready to start a new life.

Robin ended up buying my house, and that cut me loose. I was free to do whatever I wanted. What I really wanted was to go live in a cave and be alone. So, while I waited for the closing, I bought a cheap car. Then, after getting everything I thought Matzaball and I might need to live in a cave, we set off to hibernate. We checked out a few caves and soon discovered they were not like the ones I'd seen in movies. Being cold, in the damp darkness, on rocky ground was anything but ideal. It was quiet except for Matzaball doing her best to protect me from an onslaught of crickets. Her constant jumping to catch one and barking to scare them away didn't help. Our fumbled attempt to live in a cave turned out to be a failure.

Solitude on top of a mountain seemed like a better bet. I switched gears, and we made our way up to the Blue Ridge Parkway. Enchanted by the lush scenery, we meandered up to Mount Mitchel, the highest peak east of the Mississippi River. The breathtaking expansive views emptied my head and filled me with awe. We hiked to the summit to watch the last few hours of light dance across the mountains. Being surrounded by the magnificence of nature in every direction was the kind of solitude I needed. We sat perched on an enormous boulder, mesmerized by the beauty of it all.

Matzaball cuddled in my lap as the winds picked up, letting me snuggle my chilled nose in her soft, warm coat. I didn't want to leave, but we needed to make our way down with a flashlight. How could I have lived in big cities all my life? The cosmic two-by-four that catapulted me out of Miami must have been the loving trickery of Spirit. I knew with all my senses that these mountains were my new home.

The sun touched my face awake after a peaceful, deep sleep in the car. Feeling invigorated and renewed, I drove on to Asheville, NC, and got a thermos of my morning elixir at a small diner. I loved Asheville's quaint small-town charm, with its old homes and tree-lined streets. At that time, there was only a population of about 50,000 people. We explored the city and walked in some botanical gardens before heading further north. I called Robin in Miami and told him we were on our way to his land.

We headed to the far outskirts of Mars Hill in Madison County. When I stopped to fill up the car, I overheard two locals calling the county "Bloody Madison" because of all the Hatfields-and-McCoys type of stories that had happened there in the past. Approaching them, I asked for directions to Roaring Fork. They grinned, exposing their stained teeth, staring at me from head to toe. After getting directions, I asked where to get bib overalls like theirs. I figured fitting in a bit and wearing a local costume would be fun. Overalls were an easy find on Main Street at the only department store in town. Trying them on with a red gingham checkered shirt, I wondered how women took a pee in overalls. I'd have to figure something out. I took a long look in the mirror and gave myself a thumbs up. Tying a red bandana on my head and one around Matza's neck added a final touch.

Following the directions to Robin's land, we ended up on a windy dirt road with no signs. We finally saw a young man with long curly brown hair waving his hands in the air to get our attention. It was Robin's caretaker Tom. He had prepared a meal from the garden and helped us settle in. That night, we talked for hours around a small bonfire and ended up becoming good friends. Much later, Tom told me that the first time he met Matzaball and me that he didn't think we'd make it living in the country.

Matzaball was in a warm sweater by late fall, barking incessantly at the falling leaves. After all, she'd never seen any before. Soon all her clothes were so red with muddy clay that I deemed her a country dog. Getting her face stuck in a mousetrap made her braver, and her animal instincts began to emerge. One day there was a kerfuffle, and I ran outside to find her fiercely shaking a rabbit back and forth, tightly gripped between her teeth. As I watched in shock, she looked at me with blood drooling everywhere, laid the poor dead thing down, put a paw on it, and smiled at me with an obvious sense of accomplishment. There was no turning back now.

I was still concerned that the Mafia-type guys who'd harassed me in Miami could find me. It seemed like a good time to change my name. At the local college, I got a library card without an ID. And renamed myself Lostar M. Logan. The M stood for "marbles," and I chuckled at the ease of changing my name. I was astonished to then open a bank account using that name with only my library card. With my new identity secured, I began to meet local folks and asked around for a secluded place to winter over in.

One evening, Tom took me to a pig pickin' party. It was far out in the woods and was dark soon after arriving. I gravitated to the fire circle while Tom mingled with his friends. Standing by the roaring fire, I heard someone yell, "Valerie!" I was horrified. How did anyone know I was here?

It turned out to be Barry, who'd stayed in my house years before when I was an undergraduate at Florida State University in Tallahassee. He and his wife, Laura, had moved to Mars Hill, of all places. We had a sweet reunion, and when they heard my story, they assured me that my identity was safe with them.

Through word of mouth, I found a 100-year-old log cabin I could move into for the rest of fall and winter. I was ready for a retreat into silence. Tom had to take me up there, as the road was only passable with a four-wheel drive. He got me situated and had some good laughs teaching me to chop wood. The warmest thing I had to wear was a hand-me-down vintage 1940s foxtail chubby shoulder coat. Terribly incorrect for many reasons, but you do what ya gotta do. It quickly became history worn out by all my homesteading tasks. After the woodstove's chimney caught on fire and the water froze, I admitted I needed help to make it in the woods.

Not being good at connecting, I needed to stretch to be open to yet another relationship. I visualized the right man who knew how to live in the country: a partner who'd help me learn to thrive elegantly in the mountains. I made a long list and did a ceremony invoking the perfect relationship. Soon after, I met Stan, and we were a good match. My driveway was impassable, but he enjoyed walking up the mountain to see me. He was a Chicago transplant, savvy in the city or the country. He played drums with a small band of musicians I loved singing with. What more might I want?

It wasn't long before he asked me to live with him. I hemmed and hawed, wondering how it would affect my independence. Would I have to compromise? Duh ... of course! This meant partial euthanasia of my individualistic ego. Didn't I remember I had to be careful what I asked for? But I did indeed ask.

Matzaball and I moved in, and I fell in love with gardening. By the end of summer, I was canning up cases of homegrown produce on Stan's wood cookstove. Then one day, when we were picking apples, the bell tolled. I was in deeper than expected. I'd lost many a good relationship balking at marriage. Stan seemed perfect, but I needed some time to think about it. It was obvious that being on my own solitary island wasn't working. Besides, Stan and I had so much fun together, and it's an understatement to say that life was easier with him. Perhaps another staged wedding was in order. I mean, I already knew how not to turn the papers in. My private life's not the government's business, anyway, right? Before saying yes, I wrote up prenuptial agreements.

Another Staged Wedding

Once again, I did all the planning, except it was much easier this time. With a bit of dramatic flair, my costumer skills came into play, and I attired us in Victorian style. Jeff, our minister, agreed to let me dress him like Father Guido Sarducci. You might remember Sarducci from "Saturday Night Live" in the '70s. I figured it was all a drama anyway. The stage was under the apple tree where Stan had proposed. Only a few friends were invited and the reception was at home. Jeff placed the marriage papers in my hands, and the deed was done.

Stan and I continued to live in his beautiful 20-acre sanctuary in a cove with a view of the Blue Ridge Mountains. It was a warm, learning-curve kind of life. Beyond gardening and canning, I became an avid seed saver and learned the benefits of many local medicinal plants. Eventually, I became proficient in country living. Thankfully, he did all the wood-chopping and fire-feeding.

Once again, it was three years later that I left the relationship. Why was it that I didn't stay? The truth is that I didn't know how to bond. Except for Matzaball and my sock monkey Sissy that I still carried around, I wasn't available to love or be loved. The invisible armor I wore needed dismantling. But how?

I realized way too late that self-protection didn't serve me. To break through my limitations, I tried a variety of things. I took classes about relationships, researched intimacy, attempted to "hang out" with people, and got into a few more relationships that didn't last. Disappointed, I deemed myself sapiosexual. It was true that intelligence aroused me, and that worked in my favor. That is until research revealed I had a corrupt attachment style of 'Dismissive Avoidant.' To feel safe, I needed autonomy. Clearly, I had abundant issues with bonding, control, and trust. Still, I hadn't fully understood that this came from being relinquished at birth.

Removing a newborn from the nurturing environment of a mother's womb is a big ordeal. Add to that the total withdrawal from the intimately familiar smells, tastes, sounds, and heartbeat of the mother, and the result is colossal anxiety. This has become known in the adoption world as the primal wound. Nancy Verrier, who coined the term "the primal wound" in her book of the same name, says that the effects of this wound are multifaceted and last a lifetime.

Adoptive parents are so delighted to have a child, and they typically assume the child is too. That presumption needs questioning. Losing a natural mother isn't replaceable. Lifelong complications often arise, and many adoptees disconnect from their feelings, developing issues of anxiety, depression, safety, intimacy, and abandonment, to name a few. My issues revolved around trust, and it took decades for me to recognize that. The initial separation wound shatters a sense of trust and makes it difficult for adoptees to make sense of life.

Did you know there's a much higher incidence amongst adoptees of drug addiction, mental health issues, and suicidal urges? Adoptive parents can bestow abundant love but also need skills to address the core issues involved. In relationships between adoptees and adoptive parents, the wound can play out by the child becoming overly attached. On the flip side, as it was in my case, it can play out as detachment.

In retrospect, I think my psyche created the hidden mantra of "Don't get too close. Be ready to abandon before you can be abandoned." Looking back on my relationships, I've always been ready to jump ship. No wonder they call it a re-lationship. Seems that most of us re-relate over and over again. Next time, if there is one, I will focus more on the elation part of the relationship.

I hoped finding my mother might help heal my bonding issues. I turned to search again but had to try something different this time.

PART 2
QUESTING

7

ESOTERIC
GUIDANCE

Aha! Why hadn't I thought of it before? I need to consult a psychic, or better yet, a series of them. If just two of them gave me the same answer to my question, "What's my mother's name?" I'd get closer to the truth.

I discovered that the largest congregation of psychics in the country live in Cassadaga, Florida, only a 14-hour drive away. I tossed a cassette recorder and a few essentials into my backpack and picked up a new journal for the inquisition. Before daybreak the following day, I put on my "Anything is Possible" T-shirt and tugged up my cut-off jeans as Matzaball ran circles around me. She always knew when we were heading out on an adventure. We sped off ahead of the sunrise as The Who's "Won't Get Fooled Again" blared on the radio. Matzaball hung her head out the window, lapping up the wind as her fuzzy ears whipped around. Her Lhasa Aspö ancestors had been Tibetan tiger hunters, and I imagined she agreed our quest was a worthy hunt.

The old Cassedega Hotel was the only accommodation in town, and we got the last available room. It had a reputation for being haunted, and the room we got usually wasn't booked because of the high number of paranormal experiences people had in it. Being haunted all my life by not knowing who I was, a spooky hotel stay didn't faze me.

I'd long been into esoteric knowledge because secrets appalled me. I'd studied the works of Alice Bailey, Carlos Castaneda, Madam Blavatsky, Ruth Montgomery, and Walter Russell, to name a few. Seances, spoon bending, palm readings, and even Ouija Boards intrigued me. Besides my own origins, I wondered where we all came from. I used to skip school and sneak into different places of worship to feel the energy. Scouring the Bible, the Dead Sea Scrolls, Eastern religious texts, and various Mystery Schools gave me an in-depth maze to traverse. Who was telling the truth? Did anyone know?

As Matzaball and I were falling asleep, nestled together on the small bed in the haunted room, I wondered if I'd created the entire scenario of who, what, where, when, and why I was born. Maybe some spirits would tell me during the night.

We arose after having no uncanny encounters and headed to the lobby. The receptionist pointed me to coffee and handed over a list of psychics. Dowsing their names with my pendulum, I booked sessions with three women.

The first one told me about three of my supposed past lives. One was a young girl in Jerusalem. Another was a dancer in the Middle East who became an illustrious concubine. Maybe that's why I love to dance! The third was a girl named Pardi, a temple virgin in Asia. I told the psychic it was all fascinating, but I was interested in knowing about this life. "Can you tell me my mother's name?"

She lit a new candle, placing it next to the one that was burning when we came in. Pulling a scarf up over her head, she gazed into the flame. After a few minutes, she sat back and said the person I was searching for wasn't coming through because I was not the entity in my mother's womb. She said my soul entered much later, and I would write a book about it. None of this made any sense at the time. She ended by saying what I was looking for was not what I was trying to find.

I'm open to channeling, but it all felt wacko. She probably talked about a life in Jerusalem because I called Matzaball by name. Who knows where the concubine and temple virgin bit came from. Nothing resonated with me, and none of it was verifiable. I chalked the reading up to an entertaining hour with an eccentric woman making a buck with her wild imagination.

Matza and I trotted off to the open field across from the hotel and had a run around before the next reading. The next psychic said my mother's name was Ada or Anna. My ears perked up because I'd written a song about my imagined mother and named her Anna. I asked if she knew her last name or my father's. She started talking about a foreign man from the East and then said, "Wait, this is not your father. He is your soulmate. You will meet him in a few years. He is like a Sufi doctor, but not really." She also said I'd meet a large-bodied evil man with dark skin and to be on the lookout to get out of his way. The session ended when her one-hour timer went off.

She said my mother's name was Anna, and a song I'd written years ago kept playing in my head as we walked off to the next psychic.

"Anna, I heard you calling in my dreams. Strange it is to miss you. Do you ever think about me, your child you never knew?"

You Must Write

With fingers crossed, I entered a dark, fully curtained room and sat across from reader number three. Layers of fabric draped over her bowed head. I waited silently, and then she spoke in a deep, raspy slow voice. "Your mother's name is Elizabeth and I see a bonfire." My mind went into warp speed, visualizing a cremation.

I pulled out of my gloomy state when she said, "Oh, that's her name, Elizabeth Blaze." Was she picking up on my adoptive mother's middle name, Elizabeth? I asked her for a location, and she said she didn't feel her close to my energy field, but she saw the ocean.

She told me I was like a brass candlestick needing polishing to shine through the darkness. Negative energies, she said, would try to usurp my power, but nothing would harm me. A foreign man was coming into my life, and she said I would recognize him by his ring. She described a gold ring embedded with symbols.

Looking up for the first time, she said, "I see you writing. You must write." I pulled out my journal to sketch the ring and make a few notes, which brought a broad smile to her wrinkled face. Seeing I was not on target drawing the ring, she shook her head and took over my pen, finishing it in detail.

Walk-in

That night I researched California birth records for Elizabeth Blaze. I found one, but the timeframe was off. Then I searched databases and used derivatives of the name like Blasin, Blazer — you name it. If it sounded close, I considered it. Then I searched Florida public records. Next,

I did it all over again, searching for the name Anna Blazer. In the end, there were no leads.

The next day, we walked to a metaphysical shop down the road and met an interesting woman named Amy. I told her I was looking for someone to tell me who my mother was. She wrote down a number and handed it to me, saying it was her favorite psychic. I called on the spot and got an appointment for the following day.

In the meantime, I booked another reading across from the hotel. The fourth psychic was a man, and Matzaball had a reaction to him. I got her quieted down, but I didn't like him either. He refused to let me ask questions, saying he'd be in a trance. Then he rambled on, telling me I'd live a long life and all kinds of generalities he might have said to anyone.

After dinner, we holed up in our room. Two psychics had told me I'd be writing, and maybe that encouraged me because I journaled myself to sleep.

On day four, we drove off to the fifth psychic's home. Right away I said, "I only have one question. What is my mother's name?" She asked me a bunch of things, which I answered vaguely, then she said she saw my mother surrounded by water. Okay, that was two mentions of my mother near water, so I figured that had to be right. She said others in the family were there too, but no one's face was clear. There was one woman she could communicate with psychic abilities that told her my father was not there, but his name was Frank or Franklin. She asked what I was writing, and I told her it was just my journal. She said, "No, there's something else." I told her another psychic had said I needed to write, and she said, "Yes, they say you have something that needs to be shared."

I asked her again about my mother's name and she became motionless except for her eyelids, which looked like an ant race was going on behind them. After an unbearably long few minutes, she told me that the entities she was communicating with said it was not time for me to know. Not time? Whoever she was communicating with was wrong. I'd searched for too long to hear that.

I decided to stay another night and give it one more shot. I had three first names for my mother, two for my father, and only one last name. Maybe another reading would give me a match. It seemed a sure bet now that she lived on the West Coast, but how would that get me anywhere without a name?

I had a sixth reading the following day, which was the worst of all. She talked numerology and essential oils and threw crumbs out for me to follow that made no sense.

I was done. We had lunch in the old grand dining hall before checking out. When we were about to leave, a middle-aged woman with glowing wild crimson-red hair approached my table. She asked if she could join me and pulled out the old ladder-backed chair across from me. As she sat, I noticed she was wearing the same white bird earrings I had on. Leaning in, she whispered, "I normally don't do this, but I have a message for you." I offered to buy her lunch but she declined, saying she only had a minute. She looked directly at me with her wide emerald green eyes and told me I needed to know I was a "walk-in." I laughed and told her I thought I had danced in. She reached over, patting my hand, saying one day I'd understand. Then suddenly, she stood up and walked off, leaving me totally perplexed.

Matzaball and I hit the road listening to the recordings to hear anything I might have missed. It'd be decades before I'd make any sense of what I heard in Cassadaga.

8

ASHEVILLE

Exhausting every possibility of finding my mother, I needed a break for sanity's sake. Deciding I wanted more joy and humor, I channeled my energy into opening the first costume shop in Asheville. The statistics were against me in a town with a population of only about 50,000. My mode of being a risk-taker coupled with my intuition, said to go for it, and Carolina Costume Company was born.

I bought a dilapidated old Victorian house on Orange Street that had belonged to the mayor of Asheville during the Depression. No one wanted it, as the word I heard was that he hung himself in the basement after being exposed for illegally using public bond money. How could I lose for $500 down and $250 a month? It was the perfect haunted house.

Only a few months were left before Halloween, a big day in Asheville. I hired a crew with the promise to pay everyone on Halloween. We weren't even in the phone book yet, but I got news releases to all media within 50 miles. My quirky crew gallivanted around Asheville in costume, handing out flyers that said, "If we don't have it, we'll catch it for you." The plan was to make anything anyone wanted for 50 bucks. Orders rolled in, but sleep wasn't in the mix. I worked nonstop with rotating crews, sometimes catching a nap on a pile of pink gorillas until someone woke me up with a question.

We ended up with 13 first-prize winners at events around Asheville. At our celebration wrap on Halloween night, I fell asleep with my head on a dinner plate.

Orange Street's location was zoned service-oriented, and legally we couldn't sell makeup, noses, wigs, or other fun stuff. I got around that by creating a disclaimer that customers signed that said the "sale" items were on a 99-year lease. If you're an Ashevillian and still have some of those items, beware! I can still come and get them when your 99 years are up.

After that, it was time to go commercial. I bought an inexpensive three-story building at 224 Broadway for $27,000, again with a low-down payment. My crew was great, and we moved the company in no time flat. Meanwhile, I hired another team to make the upstairs of the Orange Street property into a separate apartment I could rent out to help pay the mortgage. Then, I moved to the main floor to be close to the new location, which was only a few blocks away.

The holidays kept us busy, but there were slow months. I became a serial entrepreneur. To complement the costumes, I opened another business called Balloons and Things which created more revenue during the off-season. I wrote scripts and used costumes I'd already made for characters such as the Z Kissing Bandit, Geraldine the Pink Gorilla Belly Dancer, Floozie the Hooker, and Zelda the Psychic. Again, I sent costumed characters to numerous locations with business cards that featured 'Acts for Hire.'

After so many years of a fruitless mother hunt, it felt great to see rewards for my efforts. But it was getting too big for me to handle. I needed a manager, but my control issues made it tough to loosen my grip. My stomach fluttered, like stage fright, at the thought of letting go. Trust and control issues had overwhelmed me. I spent days setting up a fool-proof organizational system. With that in place, I brought in a manager and delegated big chunks.

Things were running smoothly, and business continued to pick up. We started getting calls for strippers, and I wondered how to cash in on this with humor. The answer was the Stripping Chicken. He'd strut into parties with a boombox playing the famous David Rose stripping music ..."da da da da," swinging his hips and twirling a big yellow feathered boa. He'd strip piece by tasty piece out of his chicken costume, down to boxer shorts covered with feathers. On his rear was a little tail, which he retrieved a golden egg from and presented to the recipient. When it opened, confetti flew out and a card that said, "You've been laid and here's your egg to prove it."

Humor bankrolled us, and I promoted the businesses together as Asheville's Fantasy Funtier. We made the front page of the Arts section of the local paper many times, and we kept creating more characters to liven up just about any event you can think of.

One day I was flipping through the Yellow Pages looking for a dentist and found page after page of dental offices. Asheville was a relatively small town, and there were hundreds of dentists listed. Of course, they all needed a tooth fairy, didn't they? Surely many moms spend time in the waiting room of a dental clinic and would love to know about a local tooth fairy for hire.

I didn't waste time making a fairy costume with sparkling white chiffon and satin. Adding a tulle tutu, fluttering fairy wings, and a light-up magic wand completed the getup. I dressed a pixie girl in the costume, and she played the part with razzle-dazzle style. We made business cards with the new slogan, "Tooth Fairy—Have Wand Will Travel," and promotions began. The Tooth Fairy delivered balloons and business cards to dentist offices all over the region, and they let us display our fun promo packs in their waiting rooms. Within a day, orders were rolling in.

My crew rocked, and I got better at bonding. In the mornings, they'd costume themselves up, getting ready for our clients. We worked hard in our funtier and became our own little community. Did I bond better because I was the boss and still mostly in control? Maybe. Did I get my leadership and innate theatrical skills from my upbringing, or was it entwined in my DNA? I had a feeling it was both. The itch to go on the hunt again was back, but it needed to wait until the next busy holiday was over.

Brouhaha

Easter was upon us, and we costumed up adding amusing bonnets to our various characters. When we appeared at a big celebration parade in Asheville, things got weird when some new police officer approached the Easter Bunny and told him it was illegal to wear a mask in public. At first, I thought it was a joke, but nope, he was serious. My warrioress skills came into play, and I gathered the crew to create a campaign to welcome the Easter Bunny to Asheville. We started with a spontaneous photo shoot of Keystone Kops handcuffing the Bunny, and it rolled from there. I put giant red sunglasses over the Easter Bunny mask, and he'd show up around town pretending to hide. The large sign we installed on Broadway said, "Easter Bunny Wants to Hide Eggs, Not His Face." The Bunny peeked out behind the sign as cars drove by, causing traffic jams as people slowed down to gander at the shenanigans.

Media packets were whipped up, and news releases were sent out by unmasked costumed characters to newspapers, television, and radio stations. We had bookoo's of free promotions, and the phones were ringing off the hook. I had no idea our antics would lay such a giant golden egg. Within a few days, the story had gone coast to coast.

We sent a public invitation to the mayor of Asheville to welcome the Easter Bunny to town. When it received no response, I planned a demonstration in front of City Hall and notified the media. Young Transportation donated an air-conditioned bus to the cause, and we utilized every seat. Numerous friends, along with my crew, costumed up and boarded the buses. When we arrived downtown, there were crowds, media, cameras, and police already gathered.

Dozens of signs featuring our slogan waved outside the city building. Cameras flashed, and videos rolled as we disembarked from the buses. The Easter Bunny in sunglasses wearing a ball and chain was the last to appear. As he peeked out of the bus, cheers from my crew and the crowd beckoned him to come out. The crowd chanted, "Free the Easter Bunny! Free the Easter Bunny!"

I think it was total embarrassment that impelled the mayor to come out. Along with the police chief, he gave a brief but grand welcome statement to the media. The law, which was a leftover from an old KKK concern, was dropped, and Asheville's masked holiday characters were free.

I developed a friendship with one of my team players, Zoe. She was curious about my adoption and wanted to help find my mother. With her encouragement, I jumped back onto the searching battlefield. She was computer savvy, and soon we were spending days in her log cabin in the mountains, researching anything that might give us clues.

One night we took a break and chilled out in her outdoor hot tub. We started sharing everything we were grateful for. Both of us were mostly content with our lives, but we came up with three things that would increase our satisfaction level if we had them all at the same time. We deemed them our three "M&M's": a man, a mission, and money. We'd had them all between us, but never at the same time. We laughed under the clear starlit sky until our saturated skin wrinkled up like crunched wax paper. We became "soul siztas," as we called it.

Season after season passed as we chased the elusiveness of my mother. Sliding down endless rabbit holes, we'd end up backing our way out to escape to the hot tub. I was getting weary of Wonderland and running a business. I could hear a new calling beckoning me beyond all of this.

9

VISION QUEST

Zoe became passionate about starting a center for indigenous elders to come and share their wisdom. I jumped in to help, and soon a terra cotta dome building was erected, and ceremonial grounds were prepared. She named it the Earth Center.

My first vision quest was there under the guidance of a Lakota medicine man named One Feather. Seven of us were smudged with sage before building a lodge from willow branches for a purification ritual called an *inipi*. We covered it with blankets to be as dark as a mother's womb inside and left a small opening in the east to crawl into. While 28 lava and granite rocks were heating up, we cut little squares of cotton fabric in the colors of the four directions. We placed a pinch of sacred tobacco into each piece to set our intentions. I tied 144 of them onto a string long enough to encircle my questing spot.

Kissing the ground, I entered on all fours and sat in the west. The firekeeper brought in seven glowing rocks as One Feather poured water on them. Steam rose as the womb door closed, surrounding us in total darkness. Sweat dripped into my mouth when we began a chant and offered up prayers.

One Feather opened the door, and seven more rocks came in. We did this four times, offering prayers to the four directions.

When we emerged, One Feather said we were born anew. He instructed us to be silent and not look each other in the eyes. He led each of us up the mountain to different secluded locations. One woman carried a big bundle of rocks up the steep terrain to remind her of how much baggage she was carrying in her life that she wanted to let go of.

I took a flashlight, journal, and blanket and cast a circle on my designated site with my prayer ties. That's where I'd be for the next few days. It wasn't clear how long we'd stay on the mountain. One Feather only said we'd know when our vision was complete.

One of my intentions for the quest was to know my mother's name. On my second night, I indeed received a name, but it wasn't my mother's. It was my own ... White Bird With No Name.

One Feather was right. I knew when to come down the mountain. It was almost daylight on the third day when I gathered up my prayer ties and headed down. I found an old logging trail, and about halfway down I stepped over a fallen tree hearing a loud scream. It sounded like a woman in excruciating pain. I stood motionless in silence for a long time but never heard it again. Going without food and water for so long, I must have been hallucinating.

Further on the trail, I came upon an opening on my right and saw an old clawfoot bathtub. A faint light spilled over it, coming from a small log cabin with two ancient cars parked outside. Had the scream come from there? I'd often walked around Zoe's land and had never seen this place. Walking up to ask how to get to Zoe's, I stopped short of the door. They might think I'm a trespasser scoping out their place in the wee hours of the morning. I quietly turned to continue downhill until I spotted a familiar woodshed.

The protocol was that a second sweat lodge happened when the last person came off the mountain. Approaching the roaring fire, I saw everyone was already back. Still in silence, avoiding eye contact, I joined the circle and drank a quart of water before we crawled back into the womb. The firekeeper brought in four rounds of hot rocks again as we chanted in the thick steam and offered our prayers.

When we crawled out, I released my prayer ties into the fire. After the ritual, we had private sessions with One Feather. During mine, I learned everyone had come down after one night and slept by the fire. The scream of a mountain lion woke them up, and One Feather told them it was an omen of bravery and fearlessness. I told him I was scared shitless when I heard it and was lost finding my way down the mountain. He said I had slipped into a separate reality. He didn't explain how that happened. "Don't worry," he said, "your medicine keeps you on course and is powerful enough to overcome any predator." That got me laughing, and then he said, "You received a name."

Instead of telling me who my mother was, he said my medicine name was White Hummingbird. He instructed me not to share it with anyone to keep the medicine powerful. In my mind, there was no doubt that the name I received on the mountain was my true name. It was uncanny that the names were so similar, but I didn't share that with him.

This was the first secret I loved. My medicine name, White Bird With No Name, became part of my myth. Synchronicities around white birds often occurred, and they became my guides. It was the living language speaking to me. Call it the voice of the Almighty, my Soul, my higher Self, or the universe; whatever the mysterious occurrences were, I followed them. The synchronicities that emerge in our lives have tremendous potential to show us the way. If we set the rational mind aside, get out of our own way, and pay attention to the signs, the mystery can lead us to the truth. I was on the lookout.

Harmonic Convergence

A buzz was happening about a global peace meditation planned for August 1987. According to interpretations of the Mayan calendar, that date marked the end of 22 cycles of their 52-year calendar, a 1,144-year-old period encompassing 13 heavens and nine hells. We were ending the ninth hell, which began when Cortez landed in Mexico in 1519. The end date in August would see a grand trine and alignment of the planets. Some thought this would be an epic final curtain call.

A man named José Argüelles was focalizing the worldwide event called the Harmonic Convergence. I remembered his name from the book Mandala, which infatuated me in college. One page had a sketch of a large stone in Palenque in the Yucatan. It showed a man named Pacal who looked like he was at the controls of a spaceship. I wondered where the Mayan civilization had disappeared to. Did they get beamed up? If we followed suit, maybe I'd meet my mother on the other side.

Researching where Argüelles got his information, I found it was from a Mayan Day-Keeper named Hunbatz Men. I asked Argüelles how to get in contact with Hunbatz. That led to getting communication from a man named Willy Whitefeather, which took me off on another tangent to meet him out west before the Convergence. The journey provided me with a deeper perspective of my medicine name.

On Harmonic Convergence, I joined forces with other concerned environmentalists at Dawn Star Farms near Asheville. I set up camp next to a tree with unusually whirled branches. I didn't know I was in a circle of crystals peeking out of the ground, creating an energetic vortex. Each crystal had six points forming the Star of David. The magical landscape laid me down into a deep meditation.

Bells chiming for the opening ceremony got me to my feet. I reached for my day pack and saw a magnificent twisted branch on the ground. I picked it up like a magical staff and walked down to the meadow. Friends with glowing faces widened the circle as I joined in. The energy intensified as we raised the group vibration offering songs and praises to Mother Earth.

When the circle ended, I hiked to a high knoll and drew a circle on the ground with my staff. Centering myself inside the circle, I thanked the Almighty for the beauty of the Earth. Then, as if I were just witnessing it, my staff raised above my head reaching toward the sky, I vowed my allegiance to help protect Mother Earth from abuse. An all-encompassing deep love for our magnificent planet came over me—the love I imagined an infant must feel for her mother. My heart swelled with joy like never before, and a passion for finding my mother rose again. It was time.

Mayan Connection

I turned Carolina Costume Company into a worker-owned cooperative called The Costume Shoppe. That freed up time to search. It also allowed me to explore my fascination with ancient ceremonial garments. With plenty of examples depicted in rock carvings and symbolic art, I set out to learn from indigenous elders about how spirituality is woven into tribal garments.

Zoe was up for a trip to Mexico, so we set off on a pilgrimage to visit ancient sites. We agreed that spending time in Palenque was high on our list, and that was our first destination in the Yucatan. I was fortunate to engage two members of the Lacandon tribe, who'd come down to Palenque to sell trinkets to tourists. They're said to be descendants of the Mayans and have lived hidden for centuries in the Chiapas rain forests. Until the mid-twentieth century, they'd kept to themselves, remaining a secret from the outside world. Their long, shiny, straight black hair with pageboy bangs made them easy to spot.

I inquired about the symbolism of their white garments, and they were pleased I took an interest in them. I learned their calf-length tunics were hand stitched from fabric panels woven on small looms from plant fibers. The unusual neck design has spirit ties, symbolizing their bond with the divine life force. I told them I was researching different garments of native tribes and asked for permission to re-create theirs. The shortest elder of the two grinned wide, flashing his white teeth, and said, "No problem." I quickly sketched out the design, as they didn't like their pictures taken. They were as excited as I was about their garments and more so after buying a bunch of their trinkets.

The Mayan glyphs and symbols fascinated us. Luckily, we found a superb archeologist guide named Moses, who was present when discovering Pakal's tomb. Moses worked on the first interpretations of the Palenque glyphs and was willing to share his knowledge. He told us stories as we walked deep into the Temple of Inscriptions to Pakal's tomb. Mayan women were the rulers before Pakal became King. His mother, Lady Sak K⬚uk⬚, handed over power to him when he was about 12. Rock carvings show Pacal sitting on a double-headed jaguar while she presented him with her feathered headdress, symbolizing the transfer of power. Moses said her name meant the Mysterious White Bird. When we walked out under a clear blue sky, a white feather billowed to the ground before me with no bird in sight. I still have that feather.

At the Temple of the Holy Cross, Zoe picked up a small stone. She asked Moses if a traditional Mayan carver could create a sacred pipe for her. His nephew was a Mayan glyph stone carver, and Zoe left the stone with him. The plan was to get it the next time she returned.

We left Palenque to follow our agenda zooming through ten states in ten days. When we made it back to Asheville, I brought my excitement about the Lacandon garments to the Costume Shoppe team. We made dozens of them, and many were used later in a large ceremony at the Great Pyramids in Egypt.

I ended up returning to the Yucatan the next year without Zoe and retrieved the pipe from Moses. To my surprise, carved on one side of the pipe was the glyph of Pacal's mother. The synchronicity expanded my White Bird myth, but I still couldn't figure out what this told me about my origins. Not yet.

10

SHAMANS AND
PROPHECIES

After watching Shirley MacLaine's Out on a Limb and seeing "Watch out for UFOs" road signs, I wanted to know if they existed. My 40th birthday was coming up, and Machu Picchu was right up my esoteric alley. I met Zoe's friend Lightweaver who came to Asheville with Willaru, an Incan *Chasqui*. Lightweaver said chasqui means messenger of the great central sun and that Willaru's mission was to share ancient Incan teachings of awakening. They were going back to Peru to be in Machu Picchu on the Summer Solstice and welcomed me to come with them. I jumped at the opportunity to go.

Arriving in Cuzco, the hotel reception person gave us coco leaves which revived me after the long journey. Buzzed, I sprinted up to Willaru's home. His neighbor said he'd be back later, so I hightailed it back to unpack. Jetlag kicked in, and I sprawled out over my bed full of clothes. Barely breathing, the room became blurry. Flashes of my life rushed by, intensifying until I thought I'd die.

There was so much left undone. How could I check out now? What about finding my origins? I didn't want to leave without ever knowing where I came from. Dizziness took over, and the next thing I knew it was daybreak. Slowly, I made my way downstairs and found one of the staff. Summing me up, he knew I had altitude sickness and reminded me we were at an elevation of over 11 thousand feet. He made my dumbass a tourist drink loaded with ginger and garlic. After three glasses of his pungent concoction, I knew I'd live.

Lightweaver arranged a ride to pick up Willaru and get us to the train headed to Machu Picchu. With a thermos of elixir tucked under my arm, I held on for dear life as the train twisted around on a narrow path, zig-zagging rapidly through the Urubamba Valley. Getting off in Aguas Caliente, I wanted to kiss the ground. Willaru performed a cleaning ritual on me in the hot springs before we got up to a lodge next to Machu Picchu. Within minutes I was asleep.

Before daybreak on my birthday, we walked up to the Temple of the Sun. I didn't know if it was my actual birthday, as I'd never seen my original birth certificate, but I pretended it was.

Willaru bowed, offering fruits and coco leaves to the great central Sun. He prayed in his native Quechua language and then softly blew into his flute as the sun lit up a mountaintop in the distance and beamed through an opening in the stone wall.

When we walked out to one of the precisely stacked rock walls, he talked about ancient spaceships and the seeding of our planet. He explained that the soil in the agriculture beds had been airlifted from miles away. This added another mystery of origins to my seemingly endless list to investigate. Was being here providing insight into my origins? Maybe the concoction I'd been drinking was affecting my brain.

Ayahuasca and Jaguars

Willaru hadn't been back to his birthplace since he was a kid, so we decided to take him. We hopped a small plane to Iquitos and then hired a guide on a small boat to head up the Amazon. The native guide, Juma, spoke some English and warned me to keep my feet up because of the flesh-eating piranhas in the river.

I was glad to step on land again after hours of navigating to our destination. Willaru led us through a dense jungle of vine-wrapped ironwood and rubber trees, warning us to be on the lookout for wild animals like jaguars. He said jaguars hunt alone and can be aggressive. With our mouths shut and ears open, we surveyed the landscape for danger until we arrived at some primitive huts where we'd spend the night. As the sirens of crickets signaled the day's end, we bunked down just in time for a downpour.

Willaru woke us up before daybreak with instructions not to eat anything because he was taking us to a *curandero*, a shaman healer, near his village to learn about the region's medicine. We followed him with flashlights through the verdant foliage dripping from the heavy morning dew until reaching the boat.

A few hours later, we disembarked and followed a path that opened up to a field with kids playing a game with sticks. They ran up to see us and confirmed where the shaman lived. The kids tagged along until we arrived at a tiny stick-built home. The shaman was sitting on his porch and got up as Willaru shouted out to him.

We were invited inside and seated on old wooden slat benches. My head was almost touching the ceiling, and there was no room to get my journal out of my daypack to make notes. Introductions to each other and the powerful medicine of ayahuasca were sketchy since it was translated from the shaman's Quechua language to Spanish and then to English.

We were each given a piece of an ayahuasca vine. I held it to my heart and listened to the shaman pray and sing, not understanding a word of it. Willaru then said the shaman accepted us, and we were invited to participate in a ceremony. A few simple instructions were given, and they said it would take a few hours to prepare the drink.

Willaru said we were in expert hands and announced he was leaving to take care of some family business. He walked us outside, suggesting we relax on the woven mats scattered around. As he disappeared into the jungle, he turned and said, "Don't worry, I'll be back soon."

Sitting in silence, I meditated to prepare myself. I was comfortable engaging in the unknown and hoped to receive insight into my origins. I remembered Willaru saying to surrender to the medicine. That was challenging since I had intense issues about anything controlling me. I'd come all this way and had to convince my inner community that it was time to let go.

When the shaman came out, he gathered us into a circle and blew smoke around each one of us. He began singing as he passed us jugs of the elixir. When prompted between songs, we sipped the earthy-tasting bitter drink. Time began slipping away as I surfed the energies and let go of myself.

The experience heightened all my senses as bright rainbow colors swirled under my eyelids. Then I became one with the technicolor landscape. I felt totally free, lighthearted, and present in some larger formlessness. My inner community was in reunion with it all, and it seemed clear that ecstatic joy was the natural state of beingness. Overcome with gratefulness, a thought arose that I had chosen my path and that my mother allowed me to be free from attachments.

It was hours later when Willaru returned to get us. We followed him back to the boat and headed to the jungle huts. Willaru took over steering the boat and told us to rest. Juma came and squatted down beside me on the front of the boat. Taking off his red baseball cap, he grinned and reached into his rainbow-colored crocheted bag, saying he had something for me. He pulled out an enormous animal tooth almost three inches long. Holding it up in front of my eyes by a thin braided twine loop, he said, "This is your medicine." The bright sun ricocheted off its ivory-colored enamel as it swung back and forth with the boat's motion. Before I could ask him if he was trying to hypnotize me, he hung it around my neck.

Juma said the tooth was from a rare male black jaguar that had passed away from old age. I imagined he wanted to sell it to me. Pressing the tooth to my chest, there was an undeniable connection. Juma's almond eyes sparkled with joy as he watched me caress it. I wanted to remember the tooth as a lasting memory of this incredible journey. I asked Juma if he was willing to sell it to me. Putting his fingers to his lips, he shushed me and hopped back up to help with the boat.

The sun was beating down, and being perched on the front of the boat, still feeling the ayahuasca, there was no hope of resting. Caressing the tooth, I flashed back to a vivid dream I'd had years ago. In the dream, I was walking in the woods at twilight, and from behind me a large dark animal came up to my left side. I wasn't scared as he brushed under my hand and walked in stride with me. He was soft and energetically safe. Looking up at me, I sensed in his exquisite emerald glowing eyes that he was my protector. I learned afterward that he was a jaguar. The gift of a jaguar tooth was significant. Somehow there was a relationship to my white bird myth.

Back on land, I tried to give Juma money, but he said, "This kind of medicine is not for sale." Then he told me the jaguar would empower my visions and give me great strength to cut through the skin of what I was hunting for.

It was decades later that the black jaguar would have new meaning in the search for my roots. Even though my ayahuasca experience had left me with an insight that my mother giving me up freed me from attachments, that didn't mean my search was over.

Nazca Lines

We returned to Cuzco and recouped at the hotel for a few days. While processing my experience, I had a vivid dream of a talking black jaguar that said I'd find answers in Ica. That's where over 100 enormous glyphs over 2400 years old are only visible from the sky. Among the unexplainable glyphs, one depicts an astronaut, and another looks like an ET. I wanted to see them for myself.

After a farewell feast with Willaru, we flew back to Lima and I hired a taxi to go to Ica. About four hours south of Lima, the driver made a pit stop at a roadside museum. In the dusty back room, there were unusual elongated skulls. One had a hole in the top and a crystal that fit into it perfectly. My driver said many elongated skulls were found in that area, but no one knew their origin.

I hired a tiny plane in Nazca with an English-speaking pilot who flew me over the glyphs. The pilot thought the elongated skull beings made them, but no one knew for sure. I didn't know who made me, so I figured anything was possible. The jaguar sent me here, but how did it relate to my search?

The pilgrimage to Peru created more questions about the roots of our civilization. Did anyone know where we as a species came from? The personal search for my mother seemed trivial compared to the bigger question of how humanity came into being. I was out on a limb looking into a black hole.

Hopi Elders

Lightweaver brought Willaru back to the States and arranged for us to visit the Hopi elders in Hotevilla, Arizona, to share their prophecies. Two of his friends, Bonita from Atlanta and Douglas from California, joined in.

We traveled to the home of Grandfather Martin and Manuel, who lived on the Third Mesa of the Hopi reservation. After finding our way through the dusty, parched land, we arrived at a humble house without electricity. The elders warmly welcomed us and seated us in straight-back wooden chairs. Willaru and the elders eagerly shared prophecies and stories passed down by their ancestors. I was spellbound hearing so many similarities to other tribal prophecies.

Four ancient Hopi clay tablets exist, and Manuel was one of the tablet keepers. He said the Hopi received them from the Great Spirit, and they were to keep them safe until specific prophecies occurred. One tablet had a piece broken off, and the story is that a white brother called Pahana will return with the broken piece at the end of the Fourth World, which we're now in. They explained the inscribed symbols on the tablets and said they needed the missing piece to complete the story. I asked what they thought the missing symbol was, and Manuel said they thought it was a bird, but the kind of bird was a mystery.

The tablets were hidden at the beginning of the Fourth World until the atomic bomb was first tested. That prompted movement on another prophecy to take the Hopi's plea for

Mother Earth to the "Great House of Mica, where the nations come together to solve world problems without war." The prophecy said to knock at the House of Mica four times. The Hopi message had already been delivered to the United Nations four times.

Willaru shared Incan prophecies and similar stories. He said the Earth goes through a purification every 26,000 years. From the stories I heard, it sounded like the Mayan were the remnants of the sunken continent of Atlantis.

Grandfather said their ancestors passed down stories of fleeing their sinking homeland in the middle of the Pacific Ocean at the end of the Third World. Manuel added that two previous worlds were destroyed through the misuse of power and domination over nature. The first by fire, the second by ice, and the third by a flood. We are now in the Fourth World, with rapidly deteriorating atmospheric conditions, which will end in disaster unless action is taken with great speed.

With all the greenhouse gas causing so much havoc these days, I asked if that had caused the oceans to rise and flood the Third World. Manuel didn't know, but scientists say that the ice age likely arose from global warming. Will our present disregard for atmospheric conditions take our species down again?

Our visit continued after sunset, and I was writing in my journal by dim candlelight as they talked about the suicidal path humanity was on. We hadn't planned where to stay that night, but they invited us to sleep in their cornfield.

It was an auspicious night because of our visit with the elders and because the next day was the Fall Equinox, the day of the sacred Hopi corn harvest. We said goodnight and collected our gear to set up camp. As we lay down to rest that night, the expansive heavens twinkled in the clear, starlit new-moon sky above us.

Throughout the night, a series of images and what seemed like instructions bewildered me. I had a vision of seven rays of light, each ray representing an aspect of the bigger picture. It repeatedly wove in a sense of urgency to understand it.

At daybreak, I walked away from the camp trying to recapture the entire experience. When I turned to go back, Lightweaver, Bonita, and Douglas were walking back to camp from the other three directions. Approaching each other, we simultaneously reached out and took each other's hands. All of us had experienced intense visions throughout the night and received similar downloads. That night changed our lives.

We shared what we could in the time we had while packing up. Then, coming back into a circle, we stretched our right hands out, one on top of another, and made a pact to honor the vision. In the process, we became a foursome of force.

It was a busy day for the Hopi, but we had an opportunity for a few last minutes with the elders. When we shared the vision, they said it was given to us to carry out. In gratitude, we parted ways with our new Hopi friends, totally altered by the experience.

We took a few days to chill out at a remote hot spring nearby. Soaking our travel-weary bodies, we tried to process what we witnessed, wondering how to manifest the vision.

The next morning, at the creek next to our camp, Bonita picked up a pottery shard glistening at its edge. Douglas yelled, "No! Don't!" She yanked her hand back and saw a coiled rattlesnake a foot away. The snake had been her medicine for a long time, and she said it was a sign of her present transformation following the shared vision.

After breakfast, we hiked up the mountain. On the way, Douglas came upon a set of deer antlers and proclaimed it was his totem for our vision. When we walked back down, something hit my head. Reaching up, I unknowingly smeared a wet glob of bird poop on my crown chakra. By the time I figured out what it was, I only caught a glimpse of a large white bird flying away in the distance.

I knew I was on the right path when white birds or a feather unexplainably appeared before me. The synchronicities of white birds woven into my life continued to be part of my myth, revealing the universal living language. The bird poop was an obvious message for me to fertilize the vision.

1111 in Egypt

A few months later, our foursome had another synchronistic bonding experience. Independently we ended up involved with an international event called 11:11. None of us had heard of it or had talked about it before, but each of us ended up facilitating part of the event. Douglas ended up in New Zealand, Bonita went to Chichen Itza, Lightweaver focalized an 11:11 event in Nashville, TN, and I ended up in Egypt.

Douglas's new girlfriend's mother, Solara, was the mastermind behind the event and facilitated a "Master Cylinder," as she called it, at the Great Pyramid in Giza for the grand 11:11 event. I was asked to create white garments for some participants, and at the last minute, I took garments to Egypt.

Solara said 1111 was a master number that continually appeared to those with this code embedded in their DNA before incarnating. I didn't know what was in my DNA. It sounded airy-fairy, but I was haunted by seeing the 1111 number. More so, 2222 caught my attention numerous times a day.

Arriving at the Giza scene, I jumped into the ceremony, which lasted over 30 hours. During the day, my vantage point was facing the pyramid. The intense high energy of the Great Pyramids and the ceremony permeated me with a sense of aliveness. Sleep was the last thing on my mind. Whatever was happening, I felt connected to all that is and kept thinking about the Hopi Kachinas.

At the end of the ceremony, people went into the King's Chamber one at a time to speak their angelic name. I didn't have one, but after everyone had gone in, I decided this was the place and time to speak my medicine name. It had been a powerful act keeping it to myself for so long. To finally reveal it in the land of mystical winged deities seemed perfect.

Following candles that lit the way, I walked through the narrow stone walkway into the King's Chamber. Giving thanks and taking a deep breath, I didn't speak my name. I sang it loud and clear. White Bird With No Name echoed throughout the ancient chamber, empowering my myth.

On the flight home from Cairo, I felt an expansion of energy I'd need for what I was about to take on.

11

EARTHAVEN ECOVILLAGE

I devoted the next four years to research, meetings, land searching, and learning group process techniques. Obsessed with manifesting the vision from the Hopi cornfield, I traveled to dozens of intentional communities and educational centers to glean information that might help us.

I had just built a home and a sound studio to record my music on the Ivy River, but little did I know that Spirit would soon direct me to turn that resource into a financial base to buy our future land. In my determination, I also sold my business to free up time and funds.

Bonita, Lightweaver, and Douglas traveled to Asheville once a month to look for land, work out agreements, and cooperate on the many facets of the project. As we all lived in different states, it became obvious that a 'way station' was necessary. I found a small 6-acre parcel with 5 houses on it that would serve that purpose. Within the year, they all moved to Asheville.

Nurturing the project forward was a full-time unpaid job. Birthing the vision satisfied any thought of me wanting to have children. Some friends said I became like a scolding mother during the gestation period. I did my best in making it a participatory process because one of the main reasons communities fail is because there's a leader. That's unless it's a religious group. But learning how to manifest the project without someone taking the lead seemed impossible. Leading without leading is a skill few people can master.

When the large land tract that met our elaborate criteria was found, I freaked out when everyone got cold feet and backed out. The abandonment ripped me apart, but the force to fulfill the vision controlled me. Obsessed, I knew without a doubt that I had to go for it. I put a contract on the land, not knowing how to pay for it.

I promised everyone they would be known as the founders if they changed their minds in the next two months. Six weeks later, eight of us pledged funds to follow through with a hefty down payment on the land purchase.

The visions in the Hopi cornfield led to the creation of the first permaculture ecovillage in North America. On January 11, 1994, we opened the gates of Earthaven Ecovillage in Black Mountain, NC. As of today, Lightweaver, Bonita, Douglas, and I have remained close friends, but I am the only one still involved with the project. There are now over 75 families living off the grid at Earthaven.

A high point for me was when Dorothy McLean visited Earthaven early on. She was one of the founders of the Findhorn Community and is known for her work with plant devas. I was touring her around in my glorified 4wd golf cart and asked her if she had seen God. Dorothy looked up at the clear blue sky as her mouth curved up to a broad smile. She said she once asked to see God and was enveloped in the scent of roses. Her every breath was infused with the divine. "God is all around us and inside us," she said. God is alive right here."

A few years later, Thomas Berry, the author of *The Great Work: Our Way into the Future* and other books, visited us. We were all inspired to work even harder after hearing him say that Earthaven gave him hope for the future.

The beginning years were rough, but those memories were the most rewarding to me. Earthaven was always an experiential endeavor, and although it's changed a lot over the years, I'm glad to report the community is thriving. As I write this, Earthaven is celebrating its 25th anniversary.

In retrospect, I realize that I subconsciously tried to give birth to a large family that would never abandon me.

Circumventing Motherhood

One woman that joined the Earthaven effort was red-headed Samantha. We became entwined through our adoption stories. She didn't want to have children either and had a plan to circumvent motherhood. Samantha wanted the experience of having a baby, but she didn't want to raise a child. She interviewed prospective donors in our friends' circle and chose a healthy, handsome doctor. Plans were all set to be a surrogate for a couple who couldn't have children. All went well, and she relinquished her baby as planned.

Within a few days, the plan went awry. Samantha was beside herself with depression and couldn't handle the situation. The new parents lived next door, and she needed to move. I cleared out my house and let her move in. She was desperate to get her baby back. Samantha catapulted over the humongous legalities involved and discovered she might be able to.

There was little time left before the small window of opportunity closed. Samantha asked me to accompany her to a support group. When we got there, I found myself surrounded by birth mothers. My guard subconsciously went up. How could these women have given their babies away? How irresponsible not to care for your own creation! It was so offensive to me. My judgmental self was front and center as I looked around the room. I was there to support Samantha, but a big hardened chip weighed on my shoulder.

By this time, I had long known the truth behind the story that I came from the monkey jungle. When Samantha told the women I was adopted, they wanted to know what my parents had said to me about my birth. I shared my monkey business of how I came into this world. At that point, I thought it was funny, but no one in the room considered it the least bit humorous. Their misty eyes revealed how painful it was to hear me.

The women shared stories that helped soften my tension. I'd been sitting with my arms crossed over my chest since learning they were mostly birth mothers. The facilitator shared some documentation about the trauma that always occurs in adoption. She said the fabrication of lies never supports the inherent need of anyone in the triad. The triad of the adoptee, the birth parents, and the adoptive parents all need to process the trauma.

I'd never thought about how hard it must have been for my mother to give me up. Regressing to a childlike state, I wanted so badly at that moment to hug my mommy and let her know I was all right.

I'd come to think my birth father was a schmuck. That he'd abandoned my mother like some of the men these women told stories about. How irresponsible and heartless my father must have been. I'd always armored myself against men, and for that matter, women too. Being independent, I figured I'd care for myself just fine without relying on anyone. These women turned my psyche inside out, altering my perspective.

Samantha fiercely fought to get her baby back. Through tears, unbearable depression, and days of tackling the legalities involved, she finally reunited with her baby. After years of Sissy being my companion, it was the perfect time to relinquish her to Samantha's baby. A story emerged that Sissy was adopted into their family. As that story evolved, she became a local legend featured in the book Sock Monkey Dreams.

12

RED ROAD TO MAORILAND

A t the Earth Center, we held sweat lodge inipi ceremonies facilitated by traditional elders on every full moon. I began down the spiritual "Red Road," as Native Americans call it. The nature-based teachings made much more sense to me than organized religion.

I learned various Native American songs and picked up drumming. One medicine woman instructed me to make my own seven-sided ceremonial drum. Honoring a road-killed deer, I skinned, stretched, tanned the hide, and laced it onto a cedar frame I made. Zoe gave me an owl feather to embellish it, and a sun dancer friend gifted me a large white owl feather, telling me it was my medicine. He said it was to support me in seeing through the dark and that I'd need that skill in the future. He thought it would help me discover what was under the dark shroud of my birth.

I'd never learned to play the drum, but the drum herself became my teacher, and we bonded. She was alive, and songs came as if she was singing through me. I wonder if it was my drum herself that gave me the song that ended up taking me around the world.

During one event, a presiding Medicine Man, Red Eagle, taught us Apache ways. He led a sweat lodge, and afterward, I drummed and sang while participants danced in the ceremony late into the night. At one point, Red Eagle came close to me with his eyes glowing in the moonlight. They pierced me with such intensity that I imagined I was crossing over some sacred boundary and violating traditional protocol. When I finished singing, there was a profound silence as he continued to stare at me. When he finally spoke, he told me I'd just sung about his great-grandfather, Geronimo.

We all went to Zoe's cabin when the ceremony ended to break our fast. Red Eagle looked larger than life, with all his regalia layered over his enormous body and two big plates heaped with food. After eating, he motioned me to join him on the couch. He asked if I'd go into a recording studio with him to capture the song. I was relieved that whatever I'd done pleased him and readily agreed.

A week later, I was in a recording studio. Red Eagle took me under his wing and began teaching me Apache ways. He told me I was not ready to know the truth about my birth until I had the wisdom and skills to understand it, but he could help me. Over the next six months, learning Apache healing techniques and chants, I wondered how long it would be until I was ready.

Fulfilling a Prophecy

One day, a shaman from the Maori Taranaki Tribe in New Zealand sent word to Red Eagle that their Chief, the Tohunga, was requesting him to come to fulfill an ancient prophecy that involved him bringing a particular sacred beaded belt across the ocean. When I asked what the prophecy was about, he invited me to accompany him. He said I could help teach the tribe chants and assist in ceremonies.

Enthralled at the opportunity, I prepared by reading up on the cultural traditions of the Maori. It was fascinating to hear how they traveled in long wooden boats from their mythical Polynesian homeland, Hawaiki, to New Zealand. The Cat Stevens song "Longer Boats" played in my head. Myths from aboriginal Polynesians trace their ancestry back to fleeing from their motherland by boat and arriving at what's now called the Hawaiian Islands. It seemed logical that Hawaii was the same ancestral Hawaiki homeland of the Maori tribe.

This linked up with myths of New Zealand, Hawaii, Samoa, Easter Island, and other regions. Connecting the dots of Polynesian ancestry intrigued the spy in me. Ancient symbols from many islands had uncanny resemblances to those from Australia, India, Egypt, and Central and South America.

I reread Madame Blavatsky's The Secret Doctrine and some of James Churchward's books that connect myths of ancient civilizations based on over 2,000 ancient tablets in Mexico and India. These support the theory of Lemuria as the Motherland. The remarkable similarities of symbols, languages, and architecture of sacred sites worldwide all point to the same conclusion. The more I burrowed into this, the more I believed that present-day Polynesian customs and symbols evolved from a now sunken continent. Story after story of ancestors leaving their homeland and traveling by water to new worlds was too synergetic to dismiss.

I'd probably have more success figuring out where these cultures came from than finding my birth parents. I was down another mysterious black hole and running out of time. I set aside my investigation and wrapped up my life in Asheville. Squeezing as much as possible into two bags, I used one just for my drum and feather medicines, covering them in sage and red cotton fabric. I was ready for the land of volcanos, thermal springs, waterfalls and living with the Taranaki Maori tribe.

Tattooed

We made the long voyage in a plane full of sleepless passengers due to the high-decibel snoring of Red Eagle. Twenty-two hours later, we disembarked at the Auckland airport and were greeted by Chief Tohunga. His long trailing feathered robe and high-crowned plumed headdress was stunning. Following him was an enthusiastic tribe of men covered with tattoos. Right there in the airport, the men performed a stomping spear dance, enacting a story.

Red Eagle said this was their welcoming ceremony, and they were performing a song of a story passed down by their ancestors. I knew about the prophecy of the belt coming across the ocean, but the song blew me away. Not only was it about the sacred belt, but a white bird crossing the ocean with it. This was too unbelievable to wrap my tired brain around. Not even Red Eagle knew my real medicine name was White Bird with No Name.

Before getting a grip on reality, a customs officer informed us our luggage was quarantined. Red Eagle attempted to convince them that our items were mandated religious necessities. But the powers that be would have nothing to do with such allowances.

We were escorted out of the chaos to the Maori lodge where we would stay. Red Eagle grumbled on the way about not being able to wear his tribal headdress for the occasion as planned. I suggested he make do by wrapping his Apache medicine blanket over his head. I put it around him as he got out of the car, and it draped down covering the entirety of his mountainous body.

We stepped into a new world. Men covered in tattoos were hooting and jumping up, twirling spears like batons. I jumped back when they thrust their tongues out at me and forcefully smacked their spears into the ground. The eccentric welcoming ceremony ended in a ritualistic feast that lasted for hours.

I was relieved to meet the grandmother of the tribe, who guided me to a bed. Her soft voice and huggable demeanor made way for my collapse. After a few hours of rest, I was awakened to a continuous immersion in Taranaki Maori life. One of the customs was that guests never left the accompaniment of the tribe, so my cherished alone time all but vanished.

Early the next morning, when everyone was sleeping, I snuck out of the lodge for a quick walk. Greeting the sunrise, I headed east and came upon a magnificent tree with large twisted branches arching out from a spiraled trunk. There was an unusual shimmer of green at her exposed roots, and upon closer examination, I realized it was a pool of iridescent turquoise peacock plumes. Something must have attacked the beauteous creature and carried off the carcass. Wanting to honor the bird's spirit, I sorted through the pile, plucking out numerous undamaged tail feathers almost three feet long. With a treasure of stunning plumes, I skedaddled back to the lodge.

I snuck in through the kitchen door to find Grandmother preparing breakfast. In Maori tradition, a person cooking never turns their sight away from the food being prepared. But she peeked over her shoulder, catching a glimpse of me. I scurried away as she shook her head in disapproval.

I planned to gift the magnificent plumes to the Tohunga and his warriors. When the tribe assembled in the council room, I entered with the enormous plumed bouquet. I began honoring each of the tribe members by holding the plumes first to my heart and then gifting a plume to each one as I made my way to the Tohunga, who was the only one seated. There was a commotion and side talk, and the room fell into complete silence as I handed their Chief the most enormous plume.

Outcast

The Tohunga stood up tall, handed his plume to the warrior on his right, and nodded his head to a few tribesmen, who then walked out of the room. We stood in uncomfortable stillness until Grandmother walked in. She stopped a few steps into the room observing the spectacle of the warriors holding the plumes. Biting her lip with a deep sigh, she gave me a look that indicated something was seriously wrong. What was going on? Didn't they like their gifts? Why were these typically noisy warriors so quiet?

The ones who had left the room returned and nodded to the Tohunga, who pounded his staff on the floor and walked out the door. One by one, the warriors followed him to the ceremonial grounds. Grandmother gestured for me to follow suit.

Outside, a deep hole in the ground was dug out. The Chief approached the area and was handed back his plume, which he held out as far away from him as he could. All the other men with their plumes lined up behind him.

The warriors began stomping their feet and chanting. Then the Tohunga raised his plume, looking toward the sky mumbling something, and then dropped the feather into the hole. Red Eagle followed suit, and then the others did the same. My heart was racing, trying to understand what was happening. They then threw shovels of dirt on top of the gorgeous plumes. Once covered, the Tohunga stomped one foot on the mound and walked away. He never once looked at me through the entire ordeal.

It wasn't until later that I found out what had happened. Grandmother said what I had done was *tapu*, meaning forbidden. In their culture, being presented with a peacock feather was an omen of one's death.

I apologized for being so ignorant and assured her I meant no harm. Grandmother was compassionate but said there was nothing to do to better the situation. I went and hid in my room with the one feather I'd saved for myself. Rejection for an adoptee can cut deep, and I had set the stage for me to be an outcast of the tribe.

Children of the Mist

Our quarantined items were released the next day, and the tribe accompanied us to claim our luggage. I'd done the right thing by wrapping my medicines in sage and red fabric, so I wasn't expecting what happened next. When we arrived, all our medicines were unwrapped and mingled together in a box. Red Eagle was furious to the point I thought he might get arrested, but at least it wasn't my fault.

That night, Red Eagle performed a ceremony to undo the damage. I don't know what good it did for his medicine, but my drum became lifeless. Her rich deep heartbeat was flat and shallow.

A princess of the tribe had been observing me as I floundered my way into the tribe. Sensing my confusion, she provided some comfort to offset my discombobulated state. Her name was also Princess, and she began training me in Maori protocol so I'd have less of a chance of botching things up. Princess was about my age and called me sister. She became my friend and guide.

Red Eagle announced a sweat lodge was needed to clear the energy, and we would share the ceremony with the Maori tribe. The Tohunga ordered Princess to go towards Taranaki Mountain to gather items for the ritual and to take me with her. Without delay, we were to go to the Stoney River to secure rock beings and vials of water for the lodge. I was relieved to have time away from the tribe and grateful for the opportunity to learn more from Princess.

On the way, she let her hair down and opened the windows, telling me how women wear their hair up to keep unwanted spirit entities from messing with it and that they travel in vehicles with the windows closed for the same reason. But this Princess was free from constrictions. Laughing, she sped down the highway, passing cleared lands dotted with boulders, with the ocean shimmering in the distance. Ahead of us, periodic views of snow-capped Taranaki Mountain appeared. On our left, we approached a smaller mountain.

"What's that mountain?" I asked. She put her finger to her lips, shushing me, and whispered that we were at the entrance of the Children of the Mist. She pulled the car over, turned the motor off, and got out. As I was about to open my door, she put her hand up, indicating to stay in the car. Looking up at the mountain, she stepped to the front of the car and raised her arms above her head as if to invoke something. She began speaking in a tongue that was foreign to me, turning in a slow circle with her eyes closed, making hand gestures, and finally opening her arms wide as if to invite something in. Then she began a fast-paced chant.

When she finished, she took a small bottle of something from her pocket and sprinkled it in front of her and in all directions, including our car. Gold-colored specks sparkled in the sun on our windshield. Princess ended by flicking the rest inside our car and on me, which smelled like musty marigolds and tea tree oil. She got back in, and we sped off past the mountain as I remained silent as requested.

We ended up on a bumpy dirt road where she pulled off near a wooded area and said, "This is it ... let's go." I grabbed my medicine bag, packed with offerings for the stone and water beings we came for. Princess got the vials for water and crates for the rocks, and we headed down a trail.

An elderly man stood at the side of the path further down from us. I followed Princess, observing this elfish-looking man who intrigued me even more as we got closer. He had a pointed fedora-like hat, clothing that blended in with the tan and green landscape, and a walking stick as high as his chin. The stick was more like a wooden staff and glistened in the moist air. We greeted him, and I tried to make out what he was saying, to no avail.

His staff was carved with intricate designs and symbols like the ones I'd seen on some of the ivory-carved pendants that many Maoris wore around their necks. Intuitively, I felt he was the guardian of the sacred water and stones we'd come for. His eyes radiated a gentle, loving presence, and I immediately felt safe with him. To my delight, his language switched from Maori to English when Princess introduced us. There was something about his silver glimmering hair that curled out around the brim of his hat that glowed like a halo. His name was Koro, and he beckoned us to follow him down the narrow path to a tributary of the Stoney River.

Winding through the woodland, he stopped short of the stream and knelt at an ancient kauri tree. He asked permission from the nature spirits for us to be there. I lit a wand of sage, spreading the rising smoke with my white feather, offering it to the four directions. Koro began chanting something familiar … "Ao … Ahi … Wai … Hau." It sounded like a chant I'd heard from Serge King, a healer in Kauai, Hawaii. Princess said the words meant earth, fire, water, and air. Those were the exact words Serge used. That gave more credence to Lemuria sinking, with inhabitants escaping by boats and ending up on different landmasses. Even though Kauai and New Zealand are over 5,000 miles apart, both have Polynesian languages. Koro said his ancestors shared stories of fleeing a great flood.

Princess and I collected stones that were shining in the dappled sunlight. Once we packed all our crates, we filled vials with the sacred water. Koro looked on in approval and invited us to come back anytime. I handed him my white smudging feather, gifting it from my heart to his open hand. He bowed his head and tucked it on his hat before disappearing through the woods. I wanted to meet this magical being again. He felt like a kindred soul to me.

We hauled the precious cargo to our vehicle and headed back to the tribe. I asked Princess what she was doing when she got out of the car on the way, but she put her finger to her lips again. Trying to bust secrets open seemed to be part of my life's work.

13

THE AMULET

G randmother was lighting up her stern face outside the lodge with a torch. She announced that Tohunga was waiting for us and to hurry. We quickly put our hair up and followed her into the council room. We heard feet stomping, and as we came in, the tribesmen hooted and jumped high, swirling spears around us. They were dressed in warrior mode with kiwi feathers flying every which way.

As we approached the chief, the display abruptly stopped with a final stomp. The room went silent with all eyes on the Tohunga, whose eyes were on us. Sweat ran down his face to his protruding neck veins. He yelled for three tribesmen to bring him the stones and water. They retrieved them from Princess's car, placing them on a blanket before him. The Tohunga picked a rock up in his left hand, staring at it like his mind was penetrating through it. Raising his right hand, he waved it in counter-clockwise circles above the stone. Next, he passed the stone on to Red Eagle, who mimicked his motions. One by one, each stone went through this process. When all were set back on the blanket, similar movements began with the water. The Tohunga passed his right palm back and forth over each vial, after which Red Eagle followed suit. When the last vial passed, Red Eagle suddenly dropped the vial and yanked his hands to his chest, shrieking in agony. Two small punctures began oozing blood in his right hand. I leaned back out of sight and grabbed a bottle of lavender oil from my pocket, inhaling it as if my life depended on it.

It was as if some unseen serpent arose from the water to protect itself. Silence permeated the room as I struggled to stay present. Grandmother brought some poultice for Red Eagle's hand and covered it with a bandage of leaves. The Tohunga looked around the room with his eyes narrowed, scrunching up his tattooed forehead.

When he broke the silence, he addressed Princess. How I wish I'd had a smartphone to record the reprimand that followed. He said there was no turning back now that she had spoken the words out loud that were meant only for the inner tribal circle. He described the actions Princess had taken on our journey to the river. I was dumbfounded to hear him recap the scene. Red Bear said Tohungas worked in both the spiritual and physical realms, but this was too eerie.

Rage boiled up in his face as he blasted her for misusing her power. Speaking up on her behalf, I said I'd heard nothing, as I was in the car, and it was in a language I didn't understand. I looked at Red Eagle to make a stand, but he was still staring down at his hand in disbelief, looking powerless. The gravity in the room was unnerving. I silently prayed for divine intervention with my eyes wide open, not wanting to miss anything. I called in guides and energies that might navigate us through the bedlam.

The Tohunga picked up his spear and declared Princess banished from the tribe. I hoped I too might be banished from this insane situation. He demanded she bring forth all the sacred tools that she was empowered with. Grandmother accompanied her, and they soon returned with a bundle. I again pleaded with the Tohunga to understand that nothing was shared with me. He uttered a loud, deep guttural sound of disapproval as he scanned his tribesmen. Princess never looked me in the eye, but she stood strong. At about midnight, they escorted her out of the lodge.

The Tohunga proclaimed the sacred vow was broken, and the consequence of this serious offense was that a life would be taken. Red Eagle had told me the Tohunga was a *makaru*, a sorcerer whose status increased by being able to kill someone with the power of their mind. I thought he was teasing, but I realized a psychopathic maniac may be in control.

When we were dismissed to retire, Red Eagle followed me, holding his punctured hand. "What the hell's going on?" he whispered.

"You're the medicine man. What are you asking me for?" I said. "Why didn't you speak up when he said a life would be taken? It looks to me like you've got your first Maori tattoo."

Ritual Undoing

I hoped the Tohunga was using scare techniques to teach us a lesson and wasn't serious. But what if he was? Should I contact the authorities? Run away? Go find Princess? Perform a protection ceremony? Ah... yes, that was it. I'd do a water ritual. It was one of the techniques I'd learned studying native medicine ways. Everyone had gone to bed, so it was a perfect time. I tiptoed to the kitchen, got a glass of water, and walked out to the back of the Lodge where the peacock plumes were buried.

Finding a long stick next to the fire pit, I etched a few feet wide circle in the dirt. The moon peeked out from the clouds, and highlighted it as I drew a cross in the center, dividing it into quarters. Holding the water up to the sky, I silently invoked the Almighty, asking for protection from any ill intentions. I begged for safety for Princess, myself, and anyone else this madness could affect. Then I slowly poured the water into the cross and outer circle grooves, offering gratitude. So be it! Whatever violations may have happened weren't worth taking a life for. I sprinkled ashes from the fire over the circle to camouflage my deed. Then I scattered a few leaves over my footprints as I left.

Insomnia ruled the night as I planned my escape. I learned from Princess that the only way to get away from the tribe was to ask to go to the sacred mountain on a quest, which seemed similar to the vision quests I'd done before. The request needed to come from the grandmother of the tribe. At daybreak, I found her, saying I needed to do a visioning considering all that had happened. I told her I wanted to be alone in a quiet environment to assimilate the intensity of the lessons. Grandmother agreed to support my efforts.

Later that morning, she met with Tohunga and apologized for my absence due to my not feeling well. When she returned, I was relieved to hear my request was granted. An avalanche of emotions erupted into a landslide of tears. Grandmother wrapped her arms around me as I sobbed into her shoulder. Taking refuge in her arms, she slowly rocked me back and forth, gently patting my back. I clung desperately to the comfort of her closeness. I didn't remember if I was ever held like that before.

When I finally sat back from her embrace, she said I was to go to the sacred Taranaki Mountain and sketched a map for me to follow. I'd hike through the rainforest and then cut up the volcanic mountain slope to a clearing where I'd camp. She chuckled as she told me I'd be in The Goblin Forest.

I was offered a car, but I felt safer being autonomous. Graciously I bowed out and rented one the next day. When I left, Grandmother came out and placed a bundle of food in the car. Then she whispered in my ear that the goblins were not evil spirits. They were actually wind-twisted trees.

I headed to the mountain and ended up passing the exact place where Princess had stopped her car. Pulling over, I wondered if the Tohunga was watching. Without getting out, I beseeched the powers-that-be for forgiveness, explaining I had no intention of misusing any power, whatever it was. If the Tohunga heard me, then he'd surely appreciate that.

I rolled the windows up and debated whether to follow the map. I wanted to find Koro instead. He could guide me and know whether to call the authorities. He had invited us back, and now sure seemed like a good time. I still had the map Princess gave me before our epic journey. I pulled it out and headed to the Stoney River.

After a few hours, I was lost. Seeing a man on the side of the road, I pulled over and asked for directions. He couldn't make sense of my map but advised me to turn around to get to the main tributary of Stoney River. I reversed direction as doubt crept in. The sun was rapidly dropping, so there was no turning back now. I found my way to the area where we had met Koro. He said he lived close by, so I drove around looking for some signs. Nightfall was upon me when a kind woman walking down the road guided me to an unmarked gravel driveway.

Turning in, there was a house surrounded by trees. There were no cars, but I was sure it was the right place. The front wooden door had carvings similar to Koro's staff. Breathing a sigh of relief, I felt I'd come into a safe vortex. No lights were on, so I hesitated about knocking on the door. Surely, if someone was inside, they'd have heard me arrive.

Exhausted, I pulled my sleeping bag out to rest in the car. There was so much stuff I'd brought that I couldn't even halfway lay down. Delirious with weariness, I got out of the car and laid down under a large tree.

Earthquake

A tap on my shoulder awoke me. It was a young man and I began apologizing, saying I was looking for Koro. The man smiled and said that Koro knew who I was and wanted me to rest inside. I followed him by candlelight as he led me into the house and up the stairs to a small bed. I laid down and slept for what seemed a lifetime, like a babe secure in her mother's arms.

At daybreak, I awoke suddenly, falling out of bed onto the floor with a loud thump. Moments later, the young man announced we'd been in an earthquake, and Koro was waiting for me downstairs. I braced myself on the banister on the way down, thinking we might have aftershock tremors, and quickly made my way to Koro. He was sitting with his hat on that still had the white feather I'd given him tucked into the brim. Smiling elfishly, he told me he had been awaiting my arrival. I immediately thought he had seeing abilities like the Tohunga. "Don't worry," he said, "You're safe and the earthquake has passed." I told Koro I needed help.

Without hearing more, Koro began telling me a story of a whalebone amulet he had carried for years. He picked up a white cloth-wrapped bundle from his lap, unfolding it to reveal a tiki—an intricately carved amulet on a thin woven cord necklace. He said it was a sacred talisman passed down from his ancestors. The story was that it represented protection for an unborn embryo and would be passed onto a foreigner who would come to him ... a motherless child. He said that was me.

Being in Maoriland had transported me into an alternate reality. I mean, things happened that had no basis in ordinary reality. Life had become supernatural and just plain weird. However, one thing was for sure. I needed protection and was ready to believe his tale.

I told Koro I was raised by my adopted mother, so I really wasn't a motherless child, but I'd been searching for decades to find my natural mother. Koro raised his hand with his palm facing me, gesturing that he didn't need to hear more. Maybe he's able to see into the past, I thought. Maybe he can tell me where I came from.

As I was about to ask him, he picked up the amulet, slid the cord over my crown chakra, and placed it around my neck. He sat back with satisfaction, looking me straight in the eye, and said, "I request you wear this amulet and not take it off. This is your protection now."

I trusted him. I had to trust him. Clasping the amulet, I felt it warmly vibrating. Accepting such a significant gift was overwhelming. I didn't know how to show my appreciation. I hid my emotions behind protective armor because of my serial bonding and trust issues. Feeling safe and vulnerable at the same time was awkward for me. Bowing my head with my hands in prayer, I thanked him and his ancestors for the amulet. In return, Koro thanked me for coming to complete his mission.

I shared what had happened since last seeing him. He simply nodded as if he knew already. There were enormous gaps in my understanding, and I asked him to tell me anything that might help me understand what I was involved with. Instead of sharing more, he said breakfast was ready, and I needed to prepare myself to continue my quest. He said he knew where I was to go and drew me a map.

Koro's map took me to Taranaki Mountain, to a parking area near a trail. I traversed up the mountain until reaching the secluded spot overlooking the vast horizons Koro told me about. Smudging the site with sage, I asked permission from the land to be there. Settling in, I intended to be vigilant and awake. Despite that plan, dreamtime took over.

Awakening to the dawn chorus of birds, feeling refreshed, I spent the morning in silent reflection. So much had happened that I journaled all day until the last rays of light and continued again at daybreak.

As was typical with vision quests, I knew when I was done. I packed up, clearing any trace of my presence. Being close to the Pacific, I headed off to cleanse myself in deep waters.

Driving down, I guessed which way to go. Then I saw a small sign for some hot springs. Perfect, I thought as I turned down the dirt road. There was no one around when I got there. Making myself at home, I threw my clothes to the side and slipped into the hot water. All the trauma I'd been through fell away as I floated in the soothing mineral springs. I reflected on my first Watsu experience in Chile a few years earlier. It's a therapeutic technique where a therapist gently moves you around as you float in warm water. In Chile, I totally surrendered to the man who facilitated the process. I highly recommend it to adoptees or anyone with significant trust and control issues. At one point in the therapy session, I felt like my father was lifting me above his head into the sky and gently swinging me around in circles. Something about that was so profound. Maybe that's something every little girl wants her daddy to do.

Pulling me out of my profoundly relaxed state, my body flinched as if to wake me up. My mind took over, and I had only one thought. I must get back to the Maori tribe as quickly as possible. In seconds, I turned from a puddle to a jaguar, grabbing my clothes and throwing them on as I got into the car sopping wet. Within a few minutes, I was barreling down the dirt road. Coming around a curve, I crashed head-on into a large black vehicle.

Totaled

I faintly remember lying on the ground and opening my eyes. A man was leaning over me and apologizing, saying I'd be all right. A carved bone hanging down from his neck swung before my eyes. Spellbound, I could barely pick up my hand and feel my chest. Koro's amulet was not on me!

The next thing I remember is opening my eyes inside a ball of luminous whiteness. Rolling my eyes up and around, there was only white. Was I dead? Is this what it's like? Can I be aware of my surroundings even if I'm a goner? I felt alive but thought for sure I wasn't. The environment was like nothing I'd seen before. I wondered if this was what a newborn experienced while waiting to be reborn again.

Laid out on a white-sheeted table, I gazed down at my feet. Wondering if I could move around, I attempted some gentle movement. My body was there all right. But it felt alien like I didn't know how to use it. I glanced at my arms which were wrapped in blood-stained bandages. They say you won't faint if you're lying down, but I did.

After fainting spells, I often wonder which state was real— the one I go into while 'unconscious,' which seems to last for decades, or the waking state we're all used to. I didn't know. When I'm betwixt and between ordinary consciousness, it seems so real. When I'm in the process of re-entering, there's a deep recognition of what I experienced. It always seems important to remember, but the closer I identify with the waking world, the further the experience fades. I'm often not ready to return, but some kind of magnetic force pulls me in. My mind's attempts to rationalize what happened as only a dream consistently falls short of any confirmation from my core.

When I came back to myself in the luminous room, I didn't know if I had been out for eons or only a moment. Recalling my new surroundings, I thought my soul was in line to birth into a new body. Was I about to be reincarnated?

A light flashed, and I looked up to see a sign on the blank white curved wall. It said 'Theater 3'. Wow ... you mean this life's dance is all a drama? Is it a trick for us to learn lessons from? Do we play a role, then return to the white womb and select another character? Is this my third time, and that's why I'm in Theater 3? This wasn't the first time I thought I might be dead when coming out of a fainting spell.

I flashed on the Maori tribe and knew I'd been in New Zealand. Then I remembered Koro and reached for my amulet. There was gauze on my neck, but that's all. There was no reason to have taken it off. It must have slipped off when I took my clothes off at the hot springs. Maybe there was a spell put on me—a dumb spell—and maybe, just maybe, I could rationalize my way out of thinking it was my fault. It was the Tohunga, of course! A fresh awareness of my situation in the present time flooded in, bringing anxiety, confusion, and a desperate need for a reality check.

Was the Tohunga's stern voice saying, "A life would be taken," targeting me as the sacrifice? I wondered where Princess was and if she might arrive here too. Wouldn't it be great if we could incarnate together and return to deal with the malevolent energies transforming them for the Almighty producer of this vast, multi-faceted drama?

I was shaken out of my reverie when a young man walked in wearing white and looking at some papers. He told me

I'd been in a severe accident. His report showed that an ambulance had brought me in from a car accident with barely any clothes on. My car was totaled and towed away by the police. I only had minor injuries and was lucky the vehicle's windshield hadn't cut me to pieces. I still wasn't sure what was happening and asked him what Theater 3 meant. As he sat me up and gave me papers to sign, he told me I was in the emergency room, which they call a theater in New Zealand.

The doc had a nurse bring some smelling salts and a wheelchair. When she escorted me out to the departure area, I caught a glimpse of my face in the lobby mirror. Red blotches peeked out from bandages wrapped around my head. She wheeled me to a desk to sign out and make a call if I needed. Handing over my belongings, she wished me well and said I was free to go.

My head throbbed as it dawned on me that I was alone and no one in the world knew where I was. I was grateful to be alive, but I had no way to get hold of the only people I trusted in New Zealand. With no car and no phone, I was terrified.

Escape

After filling out hospital and police forms, the receptionist called the car rental company to find out where my vehicle had been towed. A cab took me there, and I saw how damn lucky I was to have survived. The car was bashed in from the front bumper to the driver's seat. In my rush, I hadn't put my seatbelt on, which in this case proved lucky for me. I must have catapulted out of the car, as unreal as that seemed, or I'd be dead.

On the floorboard, under shards of glass, I found Koro's amulet wrapped in a wet towel. Wiping it off, I prayed for protection and slid it over my bandages. The power of the amulet must have spared my life. It was the only thing besides not wearing a seat belt that could explain my survival. My drum and medicine bundles were thankfully safe in the back seat.

Tossing all my things into the cab, I asked the driver to take me to a nearby motel. I didn't know where else to go. The car rental company informed me that their insurance had covered any damages. They offered me another car, but I asked them to wait a day. I wasn't about to drive yet. Nor would I make any decisions until I regained strength and got my wits together. I'd taken everything important when leaving the Maori lodge, so I didn't have to return.

I had to slow down in order to keep up with everything that was happening. I wondered if the Tohunga knew I hadn't followed his instructions. Maybe I needed to tell the police I thought he tried to kill me. But what proof did I have? They'd think I was crazy. Would anyone believe what had happened?

I set up a small altar in the motel room and smudged everything with white sage, giving thanks for being alive. Then I prayed for guidance. Who exactly do I ask for guidance? It's not like a personified being ... it's not to anything formed or formless. It's the Divine Almighty catch-all. The advice I got was simply to rest.

Reaching for my journal, an owl feather fell into my lap and brought me back to the scene of arriving at the airport. Our medicines, the owl and eagle, had ended up nesting together. Owl feathers and an owl claw clasped tightly around an obsidian egg had commingled with his medicine. The owl sees clearly in the dark, and I sensed this is what I was offered at that moment, a reminder to look deeper through the dark side.

The owl is also a symbol of death. I'd always thought it was the death of the ego, but maybe there was more to it. Red Eagle's concern about our medicines touching each other may have been because that was also an omen of death, like peacock feathers were to the Maori. Somehow, I'd been a messenger of death to both Red Eagle and the Tohunga.

Had I been positioned to expose some atrocious black magic? If so, why me? Contemplating the scenario, I thought both the Tohunga and Red Eagle were teachers of the dark forces. Did I have to see into the darkness to unveil it? Eagle medicine traditionally carries a broad view but not the ability to see through the dark. Had Red Eagle's power diminished when our medicines entwined? The Red Eagle, with a punctured hand, was weak and scared. The negative power that both these men were using needed to end. No wonder the Tohunga was so upset by Princess reciting that chant. Her actions followed on the heels of him being presented with the eye-of-death peacock plume.

I recalled how the Tohunga raged through the kitchen one day because a woman had turned her back on the food she was preparing. That was not allowed in his chiefdom. He picked up pans and handfuls of sweet potatoes and threw them out the door, barely missing where I stood. The rage was despicable, and my perception of him spiraled downward. I didn't care if he was their fearless leader; what I saw was fear. Was he afraid he'd be poisoned?

Red Eagle's pomp in parading around like a big chief, headdress and all, had slowly become repulsive to me. It began when I realized he didn't have a clue about the stones and water vials. Back in North Carolina, where he had been teaching, I'd found many of the things he shared to be untraditional to the Apache ways. He said he taught children not to fear, yet he taught by fear. I distanced myself from him since the night I did the water protection ceremony.

The more I recollected interactions with these men, the more I could see how I might fit into this stranger-than-strange scenario. A psychic named Shirley, that I met in Cassadaga, told me I'd meet a large-bodied evil man. Souls on the dark side, she said, are drawn to individuals to confront things that will help their souls evolve. She said I was an agitator to taunt dark energies because I had the strength to stand up against them. She said I was out of harm's way, and the encounters would support my growth. At the time, I thought it was a bunch of mumbo jumbo. Now it seemed like she saw the truth. I'd never had much fear, and my curiosity had led me into some dangerous situations, but nothing like this. I needed to sleep on all of it. Dosing with valerian root tincture, I snugged myself into bed. A myriad of thoughts scrambled my brain until I fell asleep.

Clarity came once I had my coffee the next morning. Home was calling me, and I booked a cab to the airport. I wrote a letter to Grandmother saying I had an emergency back home and had to leave. I told her I was sorry not to have said goodbye in person and to let the Tohunga and the rest of the tribe know.

I asked a stranger to take a photo of me before boarding my flight to California. That photo summed up my experience. I had two large prominent black eyes like tattoos, and the sign behind me read

NEW ZEALAND WARNING!

A Life is Taken

I landed in Los Angeles and called Burt, my old college friend. He picked me up and took me to his boat. As we set sail, I called Zoe, who was taking care of Matzaball, and briefed her on what had happened. Right before we lost our connection, she told me that Matzaball had unexpectedly gotten sick the same day as my accident and had passed away.

Devastated, I was convinced that Matzaball had given her life for me. My chest ached as I gasped for breath. My best friend was gone. I needed to get home. When we docked the sailboat again, I had Burt take me back to the airport to catch the next flight.

Zoe met me at the Asheville airport and showed me pictures and videos of the ceremony she'd done for Matzaball. She had buried her on Paw Paw Ridge above the Sound Chamber, next to her dog, Sassy, who passed away the year before. Matzaball and Sassy had been best friends.

We hiked up to the ridge, and I laid beside Matzaball's' grave and wept for hours, praying for her safe journey into the land of Spirit. Matzaball was my family, and she had made the ultimate sacrifice. Zoe arranged a sweat lodge, and I laid my drum and medicine bundles on the altar. We prayed that all negative energies return to the source they emanated from.

Not long after, we got the shocking news that the Tohunga had fallen ill and passed away. I struggled with insane thoughts that it was because of the peacock feather or that I prayed that all his negative energies return to their source.

Exposed

I sent word to the council of Apache elders inquiring about Red Eagle. After all I had experienced in New Zealand, I doubted his heritage claims and asked Zoe never to host him again. She didn't believe me and continued to book him as a wisdom teacher. Because of that, I stayed away from the Sound Chamber.

Within a few months, the Apache Council issued a statement that Red Eagle was unrelated to Geronimo. He was a fraud. He had no authority to claim he was a chief or medicine man. Geronimo's only direct descendants are his Apache family at Mescalero, New Mexico, and the Fort Sill Apache Tribe in Oklahoma. Red Eagle was not enrolled with either tribe.

To this day, Red Eagle still espouses himself as he always has, despite being exposed. The man has exploited the good name of Geronimo and the Apache nation. He continues to take money for sacred ceremonies and conduct workshops. Zoe quit sponsoring him when the disclaimer came out, and our friendship became stronger than ever.

I never knew if Grandmother had received my letter, and I still don't know what happened to Princess. Those mysteries remain. But the truth about Red Eagle came out, and the Tohunga was dead. It was time to lay this part of my life to rest and get on with finding my roots. I could hear my drum calling again. She was like my heartbeat, and she was asking me to sing a new song.

"Life is either a daring adventure or nothing."
- Helen Keller

PART 3
ALLURE

14

INDIA BECKONS

An elder from India, who I'll refer to as Maharaji, came to America to speak at the World Peace Summit at the United Nations. Afterward, he came to Asheville for a three-day retreat at the Peace Chamber.

Receiving him at the airport, he was easy to spot. His tall stature donned a long papaya-colored robe flowing down to intricately carved wooden sandals. Silver hair peaked out from a matching headscarf tied under his chin, like a babushka you might see an elderly Russian woman wearing. We adorned him with our homemade flowered malas, and his bushy mustache perked up, revealing a wide grin as we sang a Hindu chant.

Maharaji was in his seventies, but his energy and stride were remarkably youthful. We took him to Zoe's, where an elaborate feast was prepared. He ate like a bird and wasn't interested in resting. Instead, he walked into the woods before our evening session and was especially curious about medicinal plants along the trails. Maharaji was remarkably playful but serious ... childlike but wise.

That evening at his satsang talk, I was captivated by his elegant hand movements. They had their own language, speaking to me better than his broken English. Then uncanny things began happening. I'd think of a question, and he'd answer it before I asked. At one point, I unmistakably heard a high-pitched vibrating tone. A few minutes later, a woman presented Maharaji with a brass Himalayan bowl. He began talking about the divinity of sound, then he tapped the bowl's rim, creating an identical sound. It happened again when I heard a loud bird call, and then a bird landed at Maharaji's feet and made the same call, but much quieter. I'd experienced similar things before but with the aid of psilocybin. Later, I had a déjà vu when Maharaji looked at me. It was like my dad was looking at me through Maharaji's eyes. Looking straight at me he said, "You were meant to be here." He was speaking to everyone, but for me it was personal.

My energy ran high, and I was the last to go to bed that night. I dreamt I was sitting in the back of my car with the hatch open, and my deceased father, Julius, appeared in a rust-colored jacket with Maharaji. Dad let me know his Soul was alive and well and that he approved of Maharaji's teachings. The two of them acted like long-lost friends.

At dawn, I downed a thermos of coffee and attempted to sit still through a meditation. Besides not being a floor-sitting knee-bender, my monkey mind didn't stop. When we could wiggle again, I asked him if dreams help us become more aware. He said that dreams come so you can do things without physical restraint and work on challenging issues without having to act them out in daily life.

After breakfast, I asked Maharaji what wearing orange and rust-hued garments meant. He said the colors represent the rising sun, the time of day when the veils are thinnest. That's the reason it's the best time to meditate. Daybreak represents awareness and enlightenment, he said, and those who have renounced ordinary life for their spiritual practice wore those colors.

Maharaji talked about duality, saying the idea that we're separate from each other and the world is our fabricated illusion. He spoke of infinite space, different worlds, and multiple universes. Inquiring if there are different worlds on planet Earth, Maharaji said that it depended on one's awareness.

I briefly shared stories of various tribes' ancestors escaping by boats when their homeland sank, and they called it entering a new world. Maharaji said the ancient scriptures tell of a deluge when the Ganges River poured down on *Shiva,* the god of destruction, and that caused the waters to form rivers over the earth. The flood made way for new generations to be born into the new world. I wanted to know how all the various flood myths fit together. But it was time for *pranayam,* our breathing exercises.

Later, on Zoe's porch, I told Maharaji about my search and asked for his insights. That led to him giving a spontaneous talk about attachments. He said the most challenging thing for Hindus on the path to awakening is to let go of family because that attachment is innate in their culture. In America, he said, it's much easier to do. He joked about how many Americans leave their spouse and find another if they don't like how it's going. That is typically unheard of in India. Once married, it's for life. He said I might be fortunate not to have attachments to family since that can keep us from breaking loose of our ego.

That was a charged moment. My red flags went up, and I thought it was a ploy to get someone to be a follower. After my New Zealand experience, I was skeptical about any supposed shaman or guru. Crossing my arms with my shields up, I slid back into my seat. Numerous people had gathered, and I missed much of the talk afterward. Lost in my own self-inquiry, I accessed my attachments.

I certainly had bonding issues that kept me unattached. The biggest attachment I had was to find my mother. My friends all had meaningful relationships with their families. Was I pitying myself for not having that connection? They also had lots of family drama that usurped their energy. If Maharaji said that non-attachment was vital to breaking through our ego bonds, then I might be better off than I thought. Had I chosen never to know my biological family in order to avoid attachments? Maybe searching wasn't such a good idea after all.

As my tension eased, I gazed at Maharaji's feet. His wooden crown sandals sported adorable orange toe socks. What popped into my mind was, "I'd love to wash his socks." What? Where did that come from? What was I thinking? Never in my life was I enthusiastic about washing my own clothes, much less someone else's. I thought I might be going stark raving mad.

When Maharaji was leaving the next day, I gave my respects and thanked him for his teachings. I told him of some of my unusual experiences during his visit. He laughed, and looking me straight in the eye, he said three words. "Come to India."

Something was intriguing about him that I couldn't shake. I'd never thought about going to India, but those words kept echoing in my mind. It seemed like every day, something about India popped up. A friend wanted to go to an Indian restaurant in town. At the thrift store, I found an Indian sari. At an event, I met a girl named India. The living language was speaking to me. I closed up my home at Earthaven Ecovillage and booked a flight to New Delhi. Talking to friends who'd been to India, everyone had gotten sick there. I came up with a plan of only eating things I could peel. I packed up for a two-week adventure and learned a bit of Hindi.

Imagining I was headed to a meditative spiritual environment was my first mistake. The clamor of noise, yelling, and commotion at the New Delhi airport was over the top. After scrambling to get my bag amid unbelievable chaos, I jumped into a van destined for Haridwar, which sped out of the airport, barely avoiding another vehicle. The road was packed with bicycles, rickshaws, motorcycles with four or more people on them, buses with people hanging off the back and sitting on the roof, and stinky, loud honking trucks with bumper signs saying, "Please Honk!" There weren't any traffic lights, and no one paid attention to the right or left lanes. The apparent rule was the bigger the vehicle, the greater the right of way. Camels, goats, and holy cows sitting in the middle of the road jammed up traffic, adding to the pandemonium. It was sheer chaos. Welcome to India!

Asking the driver to slow down was useless. He smiled, said, "Ya, ya," and raced on. I've since learned that many Indian males will respond to anything you say to them with "ya, ya," accompanied by their traditional head bob. That's confusing as the nod is a back-and-forth gesture; where I come from indicates "no." As much as I wanted to look out at the landscape, I closed my eyes after our driver passed a bus and came within a few feet of hitting another oncoming bus. Somehow, I needed to embrace the chaos.

Haridwar Arrival

It was late afternoon when I arrived at Maharaji's ashram. He was sitting on the rooftop giving out fruit *prasad* to a long line of people. I'd seen him doing this when he was in Asheville. Prasad is a variety of fruits, nuts, sweets, and gifts people bring to their teachers, which is then blessed and passed out to others. I covered my head and arms, going unnoticed to observe the scene. He was giving each person a piece of fruit. He hadn't seen me yet, and I didn't know if he'd even recognize me. Maybe he said, "Come to India" to everyone. What had I gotten myself into?

The person before me finished, and Maharaji leaned down and picked up a banana. Thank God, I thought, I can eat that. Our eyes met in recognition, and he flashed a wide grin. He put the banana down, picked up an enormous bunch of them, and laid them in my open hands. I was concerned that everyone else only got one piece of fruit. I broke off a single banana and handed the rest back to him. He laughed with a twinkle in his eye and handed them back to me, saying, "Welcome."

When everyone received prasad, he began a satsang. Being a foreigner, I was asked to sit up front. After a few minutes, I squirmed, trying to keep my legs crossed like everyone else. I hadn't prepared for this at all and embarrassingly repositioned myself constantly until it was over.

A young boy showed me to a room and brought a sealed case of bottled water. He said, "Maharaji says you drink this only. Now rest you." I handed him a few candies I'd brought and thanked him in Hindi, saying, "*Dhanyavaad.*"

After I unstuffed my pillow from my suitcase, I let jet lag take over. I didn't hear the person who came to my room to deliver evening turmeric milk, nor did I hear them in the morning with chai. I put a note on my door in Hindi that said, "Sleeping, thank you." Rest and time to acclimate were what I needed. Between sleeping spells, I journaled and gobbled bananas like a wild monkey.

When the evening milk came, I thought it was morning. I cracked the door, and a young boy handed me a pot of hot turmeric milk. I stirred a packet of instant coffee into it, but seeing the messy dark concoction, I didn't have the gumption to drink it. The next morning there was a knock and a loud voice saying, "Please madam, open up." The young boy had a pot of hot water and a few sealed tea bags. He was learning English and said Maharaji had instructed him to only give me drinks made with bottled water. "Safe to drink," he said proudly. After I tossed some instant coffee into it, I was ready to face the world again.

A different young man came to my door to say Maharaji wanted to see me. I wrapped a shawl around my caftan and followed him to Maharaji's room, which turned out to be right across from my room on the upper floor. There were bunches of flowers, boxes of fruit, and people silently sitting cross-legged waiting for Maharaji to appear. We walked through a narrow pathway between them to Maharaji's door. He was sitting on a bed, and a man was on the floor next to him. He was a translator and invited me to sit. I had written a letter in Roman Hindi, and now was the time to read it. Fumbling through with my horrible Hindi accent, Maharaji was pleased with my attempt. The translator said, "Why don't you just speak English and I'll do this." Maharaji stopped him, saying it was good for me to practice Hindi. We ended up conversing about the day's upcoming events, and he invited me to accompany him.

Thanking Maharaji, I awkwardly got up from my entangled yogi position. Before opening the door where hundreds of people were waiting, I looked back at Maharaji. A beam of light shone across the room from his eyes to mine, filling me with a sense of loving wholeness. Maharaji asked me in English, "What took you so long?" Breathing into my soul's depths, I realized he was inquiring not only about the time since we met in Asheville but about my entire life. My answer surprised me: "I had to die first." He clasped his hands together nodding in agreement.

The translator opened the door, and I zigzagged my way through the sea of orange and white-dressed devotees back to my room. Mesmerized by what had happened, I thought back to college when I switched from theater to philosophy and then to religion. The Vedas and other texts were all about the death of the ego. I knew that's how Maharaji understood my response. But I sure hadn't risen above my ego. After taking a philosophy of religion, I concluded it was all a drama, with each of us playing our parts. I switched my major back to theater, which only boosted my ego. Now here I was in India, playing my part in the grand theater of life, although I didn't know what the role was.

I changed into a white tunic, and when I came out again, Maharaji gave a satsang. He offered me a chair, but I knew this was not protocol, so I declined and sat on the floor. He introduced me and asked for a translator to come forward so I'd understand him easier.

When Maharaji stood to leave, I followed him with the entire crowd. I asked one of the female saints where we were going, and she said it was bad luck to ask. I was ushered into his van and seated behind him. Numerous vehicles followed us, and I wondered if anyone had a clue where we were going. Surrender became a new daily practice.

We arrived at an enormous field and pulled in behind a stage. I couldn't read the billboards and posters with Maharaji's picture, but it had to be a big deal. Rose petals were thrown on our van while trumpets, drums, and a chanting parade escorted us in. Devotees acting as security guards held hands and formed two lines, letting us get through the crowd. People were trying to sneak under the lines to touch Maharaji's feet. That seemed dangerous as he was in his wooden sandals, which are called crowns. I also tried to keep people from breaking through the lines. Then they tried to grab my feet as well. I was like a fan following a rock star. On stage, loudspeakers announced his arrival to thousands of people.

When Maharaji sat down, silence blanketed the arena. He spoke for an hour while my unyogic body strained to be still. With numerous media cameras panning the stage, I forced myself to look at ease. When it was time to leave, my legs were totally numb. I untangled myself, barely able to stand, and limped off behind Maharaji.

Every day that followed was just as astonishing. I traveled with Maharaji to many of his ashrams, schools, Ayurvedic and medical centers, homes for physically and mentally challenged children, as well as large elaborate weddings and satsang venues.

One project that claimed my heart was providing alternatives to orphanages, women's shelters, and old age homes. It was in Vrindavan and called *Vatsalya Gram*, which means the place of mother's love. I fantasized about how much good I'd do if I got involved. With years of experience setting up Earthaven Ecovillage, I had many skills useful for this project. Organizational proficiency was lacking in India, and that was something I might offer.

Street Infant

The journey beyond Vrindavan took us back through Delhi, where we stayed the night in one of his ashrams. Before we left the following day, I ventured out for a walk. A few blocks away, an infant was lying on the side of the street in the scorching sun. The baby's ear looked swollen and infected. As I approached, a dog tugged at the infant's ear. I got the attention of a woman who came to help me shoo the dog away. She picked the baby up and wrapped it in her long scarf. I didn't understand what she was saying or whether she was the mother, but I was relieved to see her take the baby. Back at the ashram, I relayed the experience to a few residents. Even though they were sad to hear about it, no one was shocked. I had a hard time believing this was happening in the world I lived in. There was no time to talk to Maharaji about it as we quickly took off back to Haridwar with a local media personality interviewing him.

Invitation

My India journey was coming to an end. Every day had been full of surprises and new awareness. Back in Haridwar, sitting under a tree draped with saris drying in the afternoon sun in the ashram's courtyard, the thought of packing up weighed on me. Mixed emotions of joy and sadness arose as I hid in the cocoon of my chiffon scarf.

The afternoon chai bell rang, and as I got up, one of Maharaji's assistants came offering me a red rose. He asked if I wanted to stay. He said it was an invitation from Maharaji. Looking up, I saw Maharaji reading a newspaper outside his room. I felt like a jaguar following the scent of the divine. I accepted the rose, saying I'd be honored to stay longer.

After unsuccessfully trying to get a refund or give away my return ticket, I canceled the flight home. At sunset, I walked to the Ganges and offered my ticket to the sacred river. Ever so slowly, I watched it float away.

Every day after that was in free fall, but I felt like I was falling up. I took in as much as possible. Maharaji taught me Hindi and Sanskrit, and I taught him English. He also supported my involvement in helping with the Vatsalya Gram children's homes. In the early stages, I created art mandalas of organizational flows to explain techniques I'd developed at Earthaven. Maharaji graced me with guidance in all I took on, and I was thrilled to be helpful.

A guru is one who sheds light on the darkness, and he indeed did that in a divine way. I began calling him Gurudev, a Sanskrit word meaning beloved teacher. I had found my spiritual father ... Gurudev.

Without planning it, I ended up staying in India for 11 years.

15

GRACE AND RENUNCIATION

My theatrical background came into play as I easily acted out what I was trying to say to make it easier for Hindi-speaking people to understand. Gurudev enjoyed my shenanigans, and I became known as his entertainment channel. One day on stage with him, he turned to me and said, "Sing!" Did he remember me singing a few chants in America? I'd never told him I was a singer, but from all I'd experienced with him, it didn't surprise me he knew. He passed over a microphone and motioned for me to stand up. Tripping on my long Indian scarf, I clumsily got to my feet. Gurudev laughed and said, "Sing anything you want." I sang my version of "Amazing Grace," and even though many didn't understand a word, I got a standing ovation.

From then on, Gurudev encouraged me to sing. Learning chants and *bhajans* of Hindi devotional songs, I'd translate them to know what I was singing. Soon I had a collection written on index cards that I'd quickly whip out on demand. My bluesy voice was unusual, and Indians loved hearing a foreigner singing in their language. I soon had a following, especially among the Indian youth.

One day Gurudev asked me to make a CD of my songs. After a weekend in a studio with a tabla and keyboard player, it happened. I titled the album *Amrit Anugraha*, meaning Nectar of Grace. I presented it to Gurudev by playing it on my laptop. He listened to the entire album, shooing people away who tried to interrupt him, even shushing me. He wasn't smiling. I nervously awaited his feedback, and numerous people had gathered by the time he listened to the entire album.

Gurudev's face was serious as he corrected some of my pronunciation on the album. He had me repeat the words to him until I got each one right. Some devotees were snickering, and it felt like I was being scolded by my father. I knew it was the pride of my ego getting in the way, but the little girl in me hung her head.

Gurudev looked around at the group and asked who knew what it meant to be devoted to something. There was a lot of back-and-forth talk, and then he used me as an example. He told them I exemplified devotion by learning Hindi, and when he'd instructed me to make a CD, I hadn't flinched. Without question, I took it on and brought him the results. Then he beamed a big smile and popped me on the head with the CD cover. He was pleased.

Surprisingly, Gurudev then announced I'd be his new assistant. He picked up his handbag that went everywhere with him and handed it to me.

Stepping Up

Being Gurudev's assistant was a demanding job, but there were plenty of devotees who wanted to help. Some, however, thought I wasn't appropriate for the position. I wasn't a Swami, I was a foreign woman, and they thought it was a joke. But I could offer skills others didn't have, and Gurudev enjoyed my playful role-playing. He called me his "*halfan mola*," his jack of all trades.

One day out of the blue, Gurudev announced that I was his first natural *sanyasi*. I knew that meant being a renunciant and giving up worldly things to follow a spiritual path. But what about my home and all my belongings? I had no intention of letting everything go. The goal of a sanyasi is to overcome one's ego and become self-realized. Me? I certainly had an ego and used it to perform and live my life. I didn't want to give that up either.

One thing was for sure, however: I'd never encountered anyone like Gurudev. My experiences with him were extraordinary, and my life was rapidly enriched. I had grown to trust him like no one before. His compassion for humanity made an enormous impression on me. But how would I do this sanyasi thing? I stuck out like a sore thumb already, and it'd be more bizarre if I was a sanyasi. Here I was again in my life, not feeling like I fit in. It was as if I were playing a part in a movie, making up my lines as I went along.

Growing up, I'd played roles to appease my adoptive family. As most adoptees know, growing up in a family that doesn't walk and talk like you makes you feel out of place. Adoptees typically end up developing coping strategies to deal with those uncomfortable feelings. You know, the "I'm so special because I was chosen" theme. Most of us don't even know we're doing it. Adoptee parents also play roles because they raise a child that's not naturally theirs.

Being given a sanyasi role was intimidating. But what better thing might I do in life than support Gurudev? Nothing came to mind that was anywhere close to serving this incredible being. He was already my director in life, and even if later it turned out to be a wacky move, I'd give it all I had now. I surrendered to the part.

Gurudev explained to others that I didn't have family attachments and had left everything to be with him, so I was a natural. He presented me with the appointed sunset colors of fabrics for my new garments, and later, in a private ritual, he gave me a personal mantra, which I kept to myself.

A steep learning curve lay ahead. I wasn't an ascetic and was never disciplined or virtuous, nor could I even squat without falling over. As an incentive, Gurudev once offered me ten dollars to do it. I practiced in my room with my back against the wall. When I sat by his side, and others crouched, he sometimes asked me to show off how I did it. Of course, I'd try, but inevitably, I fell backward, to everyone's amusement.

I felt incompetent, and some of his other devotees reinforced that. Who was this foreigner who got to travel with Gurudev? Why not them? There were signs of jealousy from his general devotees, but mostly from sannyasis. It was clear that many of them had not overcome their egos. Gurudev's proclamation didn't satisfy some, and they insisted I go through the rebirth ritual of cutting my hair and receiving a new name.

I was okay with cutting my hair since India was hot anyway. What difference did shaving my head make if I were going to bypass my ego? To the dismay of some, he announced that I didn't need to do any of that. Since I was a natural, I was fine just like I was.

Later that year, I reminded Gurudev I had property in NC and wanted to donate everything to his cause. He grinned like he'd won the lottery, and I thought it'd be a done deal. Instead, he said I was a skilled manager and wanted me to keep everything in my name. That astounded me! It was proof he wasn't in this to get anything from me.

When I told friends back home that I had a guru, they were shocked and concerned that I'd gone bonkers. Maybe so, but losing my mind didn't seem like a bad idea.

I embraced his satsangs and managed to compile three books on his teachings: Body to Soul Consciousness, Inner Peace, and 108 Insights. The last one was my pet project. I sorted through the teachings I'd recorded and then compiled 108 quotes that I found powerful. It was translated into four languages and made into an audiobook with music.

During the summers, when India was the hottest, we traveled to other countries where foreign devotees set up retreats for Gurudev. This provided an escape from the summer heat and allowed me to renew my visa as required every six months.

I traveled with Gurudev through Europe, Singapore, Dubai, New Zealand, South America, the USA, and India. Speaking Hindi, Spanish, and English was a big plus. It was a rare privilege to assist him, but also highly demanding. As the only one traveling with Gurudev, I was busier than ever. Triple-tasking became a way of life. Being responsible for packing, unpacking, setting out clothes, overseeing meals, setting up video recordings, taking personal appointments with those who sought his guidance, handling money, singing, and other things added layers of sub-characters to my role.

On one journey, we went to New Zealand where Gurudev presided over and blessed the opening of a new Sikh temple. Flying into Auckland brought on flashbacks of the Taranaki Maori tribe. Was it a good idea to return to this country? I sure wouldn't be wandering off by myself. Being under the wings of my spiritual father kept my anxiety at bay.

The Gold Box

A grand procession welcomed Gurudev to the temple, where he gave a satsang. The breathtaking temple was their Sikh Gurdwara, replicating the famous Golden Temple in Amritsar, Panjab. After a day of non-stop activity, I was exhausted by the time Gurudev went to bed. Unpacking my bag, I had a freak-out moment. I'd forgotten the eye cream I used every night. I was so busy taking care of the journey's details that I'd neglected myself. An avalanche of emotions came over me. My mind was saying, "If he's enlightened, then shouldn't he know my needs and make sure I'm taken care of? Wouldn't the Almighty take care of me because I was working day and night to support this work?"

How in the world would I get eye cream? Even though our hosts assured me they'd get anything I needed, I didn't feel comfortable asking for something so trivial and vain as eye cream. Feeling abandoned and alone, I had doubts about Gurudev. I cried like a baby until I fell asleep.

I woke up feeling ridiculous about the emotions I'd gone through. After morning chai, I greeted people waiting to see Gurudev. They always brought gifts and donations, and I'd sit by Gurudev as he handed me the offerings. The last person was the woman architect for the Temple. After she left, I did the usual thing, opening the gift and showing it to him. It was a beautifully wrapped gold foil box. When I lifted off the lid, I was beyond stunned. Inside was a small jar labeled Gold Eye Cream. Unbelievable! I looked at Gurudev as tears ran down my cheeks, "Why would she give this to you?" He said, "It is for you, no crying."

That incident made me even more vigilant about my mind's ramblings. Was the Almighty arranging this, or did Gurudev know what had happened to me? I'd already seen many miraculous things happen around him. But for me, this one took the cake. Whatever the explanation, I would never ever doubt my Gurudev again.

"This marvelous world is unreal."
- Gurudev

16
AMAZON JUNGLE

On another journey, I accompanied Gurudev deep into the Amazon jungle in Brazil. Gurudev went to fulfill an ancient prophecy of the Canamarie tribe that lived in a small village next to the Amazon River. According to Sharay, the chief medicine man of the tribe, they had waited many moons for his arrival. Their ancestors told a story that the Creator would send a holy man in orange robes from far away to clear the scales from their eyes and strengthen their shamanic work.

Sharay had gone by foot and boat on a three-day journey to get to a phone to make a collect call to Dr. Ipu in New York. Ipu was an anthropologist and the director of the Native Cultural Alliance, supporting tribes in remote areas. He had worked with the Canamarie tribe many times in the past. Sharay told Ipu that the tribe had a vision of the holy one in orange robes coming to their village.

Ipu was a friend of Debbie, a devotee of Gurudev's from Long Island. He'd recently visited her home and was captivated by a framed photograph of Gurudev. Upon hearing Sharay's story, Ipu described the picture and told him that the coincidences all pointed to Gurudev being the one they'd had ceremonial visions of. Sharay asked Ipu to humbly request Gurudev to come with him on his upcoming trip to the Amazon.

That sounded like a wild story, but after being with Gurudev for a few years and witnessing so many miraculous things, I knew it had to have some cosmic reality behind it. Gurudev accepted the request to go, and plans were made.

We flew into São Paulo and then on to Manaus. After a brief rest, we boarded a small boat to the confluence where the Black River's dark waters mingled with the Amazon's golden flow. We ceremonially honored the Goddess of Water, *Yara*, with an offering of fruits prepared by Ipu, a shaman himself.

Indian and Brazilian cultures were alike in making offerings when going to a confluence of two rivers. Gurudev said when two mighty powers like this meet or the goddesses of the Ganges and Yamuna rivers merge, there's a third hidden sacred power that sanctifies the union. Like in the mundane world, wherever there is a union of two, there's always the unseen third power of divinity. We remain in duality if we don't remember the third part of the union.

My mind dropped into a fantasy that I was the unseen divine power generated by my birth parent's union. They had to remember me, even though they let me go. But no sooner than I felt a bit divine, I was lured back into duality.

Gurudev emphasized the reason humans are born is to understand this third power. He said, "Everyone has the ability to rise above duality and witness the sacred power of the Trinity."

After the ceremony, we traveled 40 kilometers upriver to the Taruma Sanctuary on the banks of the Black River. Chief Sharay and his tribe and healers from other villages were gathered when our boat arrived. Rattles were shaking as the group chanted an Amazonian welcoming song. A blue feathered headdress perched above Chief Sharay's painted face bent low as Gurudev disembarked. As Sharay stood up, I saw a black jaguar painted on his rectangular loincloth.

The chief of a neighboring tribe grinned and mimicked Gurudev's greeting of pressing his palms together in front of his chest and lowering his head in the traditional Hindu way of saying *namaste*, which means I honor the divinity within you. On his belly was a large painting of an ant, which designated his tribe. Everyone had red, white, and black symbols painted on them and adornments of feathers, cowry shells, and seeds. The women, who typically never wore tops, had little triangular fabric cutouts partially covering their breasts. Their short grassy skirts swayed to the melody of the welcome song. Ipu requested everyone's 'privates' be covered in respect of the Hindu culture, and it was humorous to see how they'd done that. Some only had a piece of tree bark or a leather thong, which was overdressing in their culture.

Their native language was *Tupé*, and with the help of translators, the conversations went from Tupé to Portuguese to Spanish to English to Hindi. By the time a dialogue had gone back and forth, it was translated eight times.

Chief Sharay said something to the effect that from this day forward, their tribe would celebrate with the stars and the moon because the holy one had finally come. They escorted us into a sanctuary where little thatch-roofed huts were prepared for us. The tribe fed us a luscious dinner of local roots, veggies, and bananas roasted over an open fire. Afterward, as the moon peeked through the trees, we joined the villagers dancing and singing around a fire circle.

In the morning, they gave us ritual Goddess Yara baths. The preparations had begun on our arrival. The water was ceremoniously prepared with medicinal herbs and oils and set out all night under the moonlight. We entered a circle of healers as they waved palm fronds, and Sharay chanted a cleansing song. Then the healers began blowing smoke into our ears and rubbing us down with sacred water. Sharay said the bath protected us from negative energy. I hoped that included not being dive-bombed by the gigantic bugs that had kept us up most of the night.

A stream of people came throughout the day to be in the presence of Gurudev and receive healing. We witnessed shamans treating multitudes of ailments, including cancer. Sharay said it was Spirit that worked through their hands and the medicines of the jungle. When people entered altered states of consciousness believing they'd heal, it opened the door to psychological healing, which affected their physical body.

They asked Gurudev to speak about his connection to the spirit world. Removing his orange headscarf, Gurudev tied a knot at both ends and one in the middle. He used the analogy of the many cultures and religions being different knots in the cloth, but the many paths led to one truth. You can tie many knots with one piece of fabric, but it does not divide them from the whole. He spoke of the importance of faith in the supreme and how that was vital in all physical and spiritual healing. He said illnesses sometimes assist people in getting on a spiritual path. When one feels defeated in the material world, one is more likely to seek the truth.

The children were loving and curious, lining up to hug him and ask questions. One child asked why he wore an orange robe, and he explained that when you take renunciation vows, you take on the color of fire because everything you've known before goes into the fire, and then life is like a burning flame where nothing can remain stuck to you. He related his teachings in simple ways they could understand.

A native elder said Gurudev made the truth clear like water and easy to drink.

The next day, Sharay led us to the Jaguar path, where they did a protection ceremony for our journey further upriver. The tribal people said that evil spirits sometimes come to break things up when holy people gather together. They performed a ritual to protect us using rattles, incense, and smoke, much like in the Native American tradition. A few of the boys were trained in listening for spirits and were on their knees with their ears to the ground, vigilant for any evil that might arrive. The older men stomped the ground with their feet to call in good spirits.

When the chief declared the path was clear, we followed him through the damp lush foliage to the small boat waiting to take us onward. We traveled for hours up the humongous river, passing many islands and stopping to visit a few villages on our way. We finally docked in a remote area. From there, we went by foot deep into the rainforest on the path to "The Angel That Has Fallen," an ancient sacred grandmother tree where we offered prayers.

Gurudev was quite at home in the jungle and delighted in learning about medicinal plants and healing modalities from the native people. His guru had been a healer and passed down ancient medicine ways of his lineage to Gurudev.

Just before nightfall, we set up camp. Ipu brought a new tent for Gurudev, the Taj Mahal of our makeshift settlement. After a meal of roasted roots, the rest of us nestled into our hammocks, which fortunately had mosquito nets.

The next day was the Spring Equinox. We traveled further north on the river to visit the small village of Sao Thome, where Gurudev blessed a school. The kids ran up and hugged him and then performed a dance. They were especially curious about his facial hair since their people had none. Gurudev let the children play with his beard, and they giggled, pulling it up and peeking under it.

After handing out treats to the children, we traveled to the *Rainha da Floresta*, The Queen of the Forest, to see how some ancient traditional healing plants are made into elixirs. Gurudev was asked to partake in a ceremony using the sacred vine of the jungle, Ayahuasca. The shamans explained it induced visions and heightened awareness. It totally surprised me that Gurudev agreed to take part.

Traditional Ceremony

That night, we participated in their ceremony, with people singing prayer songs for seven hours while drinking numerous glasses of medicinal Ayahuasca. This was different from the time I had taken the elixir in Peru. Here we were in a church-like setting. Men were on one side and women on the other. After singing a song, people walked up to an altar and were handed a cup of medicine. This continued until almost daybreak. I lost count, but most people, including me, had over six doses during the ceremony.

The night was an intensely personal purification for me, but exactly how to describe it is beyond words. My insides turned inside out and expanded beyond me. After emptying whatever needed purging, all my senses heightened and mingled, creating some new faculty. At times there was no separation of being in or out of my body. I was aware that I, or something bigger than myself, chose the life I was living. It all seemed clear at the time.

The next afternoon, we had a debriefing. People had varying extraordinary experiences, some blissful and some repugnant. Gurudev said it was natural that we had different experiences because it depended on our nature and faith. He said, "If your nature is to worry, then you may experience that, and if you think you will have profound insights, then the event will unfold like that."

He explained that faith is essential but is different for a child, a youth, or an elder. For example, if Gurudev spoke from a logical intellectual standpoint, then those with a rational nature might be convinced. But if a guru offers a disciplined practice, students might not get into that. But if a guru shows them miracles, they're more interested. Some people are only persuaded by magic. Sai Baba is an Indian saint who performs miracles, breaks through logical thought, and instills faith in intellectuals and children alike. Gurudev said these miracles are unnecessary for a spiritual path, but if it is conducive to the person's evolution, so be it. He said natural medicines like Ayahuasca help some seekers open to realms they haven't experienced before. But humans do have the ability to access higher realms of consciousness without magic tricks or medicine.

Thunder rolled in as I wondered if the miracles that I'd witnessed with Gurudev were something he did to increase my faith. A bright flash of lightning that hit close to us exclaimed yes. Gurudev said seeing lights or having something appear spontaneously is a lure, but eventually one moves beyond these things. There is no greater miracle than to keep ourselves free from inner worries and outside impurities. Our spiritual journey of heightened awareness ends in true knowledge when we do that.

I asked Gurudev to share what the Ayahuasca ceremony had been like for him. He simply said he hadn't experienced anything unusual. That was hard to believe. I think it didn't affect him because he already lived in a state of uninterrupted awareness.

The following day, we packed up early to leave. When we arrived at the dock, the entire tribe awaited us. The shamans thanked Gurudev, saying he had been a divine agent in removing their blinders and increasing their visionary healing powers. His benevolence, they said, allowed them to learn from his example, and now whether they were near or far from his physical form, they would continue to grow through his teachings. Everyone was hugging and teary-eyed except Gurudev. He always seemed so centered and unemotional, except for laughing episodes.

As we cast off, Sharay shouted, "We will tell the story of our prophecy being fulfilled for many generations to come." The tribe waved and chanted, "*Aba abare*," meaning "May the Creator bless you," until we could no longer hear them.

Discretion

We traveled back to Manaus and spent the night by ourselves in actual beds. So much had happened, and we all needed some self-care time to process. We spent the last day at the sacred caves near the Iracema waterfalls. Ipu had us write prayers on leaves, and we burned incense in the caves as part of an "*Edeyapá*" ceremony honoring Mother Earth. The ceremony ended with a purification under the waterfall.

We all knew to dress discreetly around Gurudev. It was amusing to see little girls in the tribe wearing bra-type tops their mothers had made for our arrival. One sweet girl posed for pictures with her triangle nipple covers up near her shoulders. She didn't know what was supposed to be hidden.

As we walked up to the falls, two blonde Russian women unexpectedly appeared in itsy-bitsy bikinis with only thong straps on their voluptuous buttocks. They ran up to Gurudev with boob-bouncing glee and asked me to take their picture with him. I was feeling like a useless assistant, with Gurudev having partaken of hallucinating elixirs and now posing with mostly nude models.

When the girls ran off, I told Gurudev that it had been an illusion and to forget it had ever happened. Gurudev laughed and said, "Our nature is like water. The nature of it is to stay cool at room temperature, just as our true nature is liberation. But like water that warms up on the fire, we are affected by the mundane world. When hot water is removed from the fire, it returns to its natural state. So too our true nature is liberated when we remove desires that keep us attached to this world."

We left the falls in time to return to Manaus for Gurudev's live interview on Global Television and an evening satsang at the Taj Mahal Hotel. Before we caught our flight, Gurudev inaugurated the Prem Prakash Ashram, a new temple for the local Hindu community. It was adorned with pictures of all the major Hindu deities and now a portrait of Gurudev.

Life was moving so fast that there was little time to assimilate or savor experiences. I needed to allow each moment to carry me. When we returned to India, things escalated even more.

17
KUMBHA MELA

The largest spiritual gathering in the world was coming up. The festival happens once every four years and rotates between four sites where, according to ancient texts, the *amrit*, the elixir of immortality, spilled from a pot into four sacred rivers. This year, the *Kumbha Mela* was in Haridwar.

I'd been to one in Ujjain in 2004, and the magnitude and chaos of the festival was unbelievable. The first time I walked out of the ashram encampment, I was stopped in my tracks by swarms of naked, dreadlocked sadhus running by. I had to jump back to keep my distance from their swinging spears. Clouds of dust and marijuana smoke permeated the air to the point where I wasn't sure what was before me. They kept coming. I'm not kidding when I say there were thousands of them.

Their gray skin color, I found out, was a coating of ashes. When I told Gurudev what I'd seen, he laughed and said it was better not to venture out unattended. He informed me these were *Naga Sadhus*, and typically they didn't appear in public except for Kumbha festivals. They are warriors who've chosen not to have family and are kind of a secret society. They carry tridents like their god Shiva, along with swords and spears, to be ready for battle at any time. I wondered if not having family created their guarded warrior edge. I'd chosen not to have children, and my parents were gone. Maybe that affected me being so armored and warrior-like. Thankfully, Gurudev was helping me let some of my shields fall away. Feeling safe under his wings, I stayed close to him after that.

Every day was intense, starting with a walk to the river at daybreak. Throngs of his devotees vied to be next to him as he left our camp. The highest-ranked saints inevitably were in the first rows of the sea of saffron colors, while others followed. If I fell behind due to the shoving around, Gurudev stopped and looked back, motioning me forward. The mass of bodies parted as I came forward. He cared for me like a father would a child in a foreign land. Being awestruck became my normal state for years to come.

Foreigners in a Strange Land

Some friends who'd seen my photos of that Kumbha and foreign devotees of Gurudev had asked about coming to India for the 2010 Kumbha Mela in Haridwar. I was a pretty good organizer and thought it'd be doable. With Gurudev's encouragement, I focalized groups of foreigners coming for a retreat during the Mela. It became a full-time job preparing for all the arrivals. But that was the easy part.

Can you imagine trying to keep track of a bunch of foreigners who don't know Hindi mingling with a crowd of over ten million people? OMG, what was I thinking? Besides that, many of them didn't heed my precaution in the materials I sent out beforehand that they only eat food from the ashram, which was strictly supervised.

They did, however, get the hint about bringing chocolate to their host. I met each flight and was gifted all kinds of scrumptious gratifications. Nothing exquisite like this had tantalized my tastebuds for a long time because India's chocolates were awful. I devoured the sweets between each flight, and the next day I was sick in India for the first time. I overdosed on chocolates. I kept on as planned, high-wired with chocolate but dragging my feet.

After traveling from Delhi together, we settled into the Haridwar ashram. Then en masse, we gave our respects to Gurudev. He welcomed us with chai and said dinner was ready. If we wanted, we could go to the Ganges River ritual before retiring for the night. *Aarti* is a ritual that happens all over India. In Haridwar, there's a sunset and sunrise Aarti where people wave flaming lights and sing to *Maa Ganga*, the goddess of the renowned sacred river.

After a large ashram meal for those of us who could eat, we walked across from the ashram to the river. Bells were clanging as people waved flaming brass lamps in the air and sang chants. Kids were selling adorable little leaf bowls they'd made and told us we had to have one to do our own ritual. The bowls had leaves tooth-picked together, holding cotton wicks soaked in ghee surrounded by roses, marigold petals, and chunks of crystal sugar. We bought all the children had, delighting them to no end. We set our intentions, lit our wicks, held them to the sky, and then scooted them into the river like tiny boats. Watching hundreds of lights flickering away down the Ganges is a sight to behold.

Returning to the ashram, Gurudev said we'd best get some sleep because the temple bells ring right before daybreak. In our rooms, pots of hot turmeric milk awaited us. Everyone was already exhausted and quickly fell into dream time.

Earplugs were no deterrent to the early morning clamoring of bells. Even with a double set of plugs and head wraps, quiet was not in the forecast. Most of us made it to a meditation and yoga session before the next set of bells called us to breakfast. Bananas, yogurt, and chai were devoured as another unpredictable day ensued.

Gathering in the courtyard for a check-in, the foreigners looked goofy in tunics, turbans, and an array of long scarfs dragging on the ground. We were already slaphappy when a camel strolled into the ashram and walked right by us. On its back was an enormous pile of potatoes roped on with jute. As cameras were flashing, he strutted to the kitchen entrance, tweaked his nose, sat down, and then let out a loud call. Clearly, he knew what he was doing. Two young men came to unload him and gave him a bucket of greens and water. After gulping up the treats, he gallivanted back out of the ashram on his own.

I mandated a buddy system and insisted no one follow the camel's lead by leaving the ashram alone. I thought I had the best possible plans to keep us safe. The foreigners were wholeheartedly into the environmental project I was working on to protest and ban plastic bags at the Kumbha Mela. Gurudev was supportive and had hundreds of large fabric banners made in Hindi and English that said, "Say No to Plastic Bags." I had thousands of backpacks printed with the slogan to give to people that took a vow not to use them. Making up a chant for the protest, I taught it to the group in English and Hindi while we painted signs with the slogan, "Ban plastic bags and love your Mother Ganga."

The morning of the protest, we gathered at the ashram's entrance. The tallest foreigner was positioned at the front, holding a tall bamboo pole with a bunch of peacock feathers attached to the top so everyone could see him. Despite this, a few people got lost in all the chaos, and there was no way to find them. I was anxious for the rest of the day because people had been trampled at Kumbha Melas.

Keeping up with Gurudev on the long walk in the blazing sun was challenging, and he was the only one barefooted. As we approached our destination, lines formed on either side of Gurudev to shield him from the millions of people gathered to witness the event at *Har Ki Pauri*. This is where the amrit, the nectar, spilled into the Ganges River. On this auspicious day, they said a dip into the river at this ceremonial place in Haridwar cleansed the soul. Gurudev was the head of the Niranjani Akhara, and this year he was the one who would take the first sacred bath.

As he stepped into the river, the sound of millions of people cheering was ear-piercing. Gurudev scooped water in his hands and held it to the sky, vowing not to use plastic bags. His voice boomed over loudspeakers as he beseeched the crowd to do the same. As he climbed out of the river, the crowd vied to follow his lead. As people took their vows, we passed out thousands of backpacks and other tokens. It was a major accomplishment to have plastic bags banned in Haridwar. Petitions to forbid them in the entire state of Uttarakhand were now on the table.

Protests for Mother Earth

There was also the serious environmental issue of damming the Ganges River. The Himalayans were already experiencing alarming repercussions from climate change, much more than anywhere else in the world. Glaciers were melting rapidly, impacting hydropower plants and stressing the dams. A United Nations climate change report showed that after the enormous initial flow of melting waters, the entire flow would stop by 2030, except during monsoon season.

The Tehri Dam, upriver from Haridwar, is the tallest in India. It had already flooded many villages and impacted farmers who depended on the river to irrigate crops. For most farmers, hooking up to the grid wasn't affordable. Not only that, but they built the dam near a fault zone where a 6.8 magnitude earthquake had already occurred. If the dam broke open, the crops and homes of over half a million people would submerge. Critical habitats and species along the river were already at risk of extinction because of existing hydropower projects. Despite this, hundreds of dams were scheduled in the state of Uttarakhand alone.

1500 miles of the Ganges River from the Himalayas to the Bay of Bengal were at risk. The promise of hydropower didn't justify her desecration. Outcries from environmental and social justice activists escalated at the Kumbha Mela as Gurudev emphasized the importance of stopping dam construction.

Baba Ram Dev, a prominent yogi devotee of Gurudev, was a respected environmental activist in the political arena. He'd worked for years on the issue and had an impact on those in power. He convinced them that the consequences of more damming would be catastrophic. Protest finally led the Environmental Minister, Jairam, to cancel more dam construction on the upper parts of the Ganges.

Having a foreigner fight for the Ganges was unusual. The media ate me up because I could express myself in Hindi. Our efforts culminated in successfully stopping the construction of the dam. A letter of acclaim for our endeavors came from the state's chief minister. I am forever grateful to Gurudev for his abundant support. Having played a part in making such a big difference on the environmental front surely would have made my adoptive and birth parents proud of me.

Ram Dev came by the ashram and honored me by taking his *rudraksha mala* off his neck and placing it around mine. The 108 seed pods are from the sacred *rudraksha* tree and are called the Eyes of Shiva. Shiva's known as the hunter or destroyer. I was a hunter for truth, and the mala was an awesome addition to my medicine. I didn't realize at the time how important that mala would become.

Focalizing foreigners was a risky endeavor. Those lost in the shuffle had harrowing experiences, but everyone was alive. They all had outrageous stories to take home and were grateful to have been a part of such an enormous undertaking. Photos don't capture what happened, but among the foreigners was Anette from Amsterdam, who was a documentary filmmaker. To watch the film, search the net for "Kumbha Mela 2010, Say No to Plastic Bags."

18

ANCIENT BRIGHU ASTROLOGY

After the Kumbha Mela, Anette and her friend Doreen accompanied me on a quest to get a *Brighu* reading. I'd never heard of them until my friend Alan Muskat in Asheville asked if I'd take his astrological chart to a Brighu priest in India.

I was never interested in astrology since I didn't know what day or even year I was born. I was free, without being pigeonholed into a zodiac sign. That helped me not only color outside the box but live outside the box and question reality. However, Alan's request enticed me with the mystery of the Brighu readings.

The story was that Brighu, mentioned in the Bhagavad Gita, was a sage who lived in the Himalayas during the Vedic period over 10,000 years ago. He scripted uncountable prophecies about the lives of millions who would access them in the future. The ancient texts were written on palm leaves and compiled into the "*Brighu Samhita*." It all sounded far-fetched, but I trusted Alan's sincerity.

There was little to find on the internet. The custom imposed on the keepers of the ancient documents was that they weren't to take money for giving readings. So, it's no wonder there wasn't a yellow brick road to follow. The original scripts were said to be hidden in Tibet. Duplicates passed down through ancestral lineage are presently in the care of a handful of priests in northern India.

After sorting through a maze of informational trails, I found the names of two priests, or pandits as they call them, in Hoshiarpur, Punjab. There was no address or phone number to go by, but Anette, Doreen, and I took off anyway. We booked a train to Chandigarh, the nearest city to Hoshiarpur. My friend Puneet Sachdeva, who lived there, put us up for the night and arranged for a driver to take us the following day on the three hour journey to Hoshiarpur. We didn't know where we'd go when we got there.

On the way, a devotee of Gurudev's, Krishna Jain, called me from Mumbai out of the blue. I hadn't talked to him since he'd been my translator in Haridwar years before, and I never knew he was from Hoshiarpur. Krishna knew about Brighu and gave me a few names, although he didn't have contact info. "There are many fake pandits." he said, "You need to be careful." He told our driver where to find the only decent hotel and wished us luck.

We found the small funky hotel on the main street and checked in for a few nights. I asked locals where to find Brighu pandits and scribbled down vague directions to three of them. Two matched the names I already had. My plan was to meet all three and then decide what to do.

We hired a local driver and set off on the quest. The first pandit we found was asking for money within a few minutes after arriving. I said we might return the next day. The second pandit felt energetically strange, and we all were uncomfortable with him. I also told him we might be back the next day. The third one was Pandit Trivedi. He wasn't home, but his son said to return in an hour.

We returned and were ushered into their home temple. A couple arrived for a reading, and the man shared some amazing stories in his broken English of his experiences with Trivedi 20 years ago. Then a Sikh family came in, and their son sat beside me. He spoke good English and said they'd come because they were destined to be here when we were. In fact, they'd prepared lunch for us. What? I immediately thought everyone in the room was a pre-arranged setup for us.

Finally, Trivedi arrived and apologized for keeping us waiting. Asking for our charts, I told him I had one for a friend in the U.S., but I didn't have one as I didn't know when I was born. Trivedi gathered everyone's charts and said he'd return soon. I imagined he was going to make up some stuff based on astrology.

An old saint came into the room with a handful of flowers, set it on the altar, and left. The Sikhs offered us the food and said it would be a great honor for them if we accepted it. I made eye contact with Anette and Doreen, indicating we should be careful. This could be a decoy. I pretended to eat a bite but hid it in my bandana. They asked us questions, but I shared nothing pertinent, as the detective in me wondered if Trivedi could hear us. I kept looking around the room for any surveillance equipment.

Within 15 minutes, Trivedi returned with a stack of old files. I asked permission to record everything, and Anette was ready with her camera. Trivedi motioned for the couple to come closer and began with them. With eyes closed,

Trivedi prayed as he held the stack of files in his lap and then chose a document. In their reading, it said, "Foreigners will be present at the time of your reading." I thought that this was another setup.

Next, he motioned for us. He did the same type of prayer as before and sorted through the old stack of files, gently picking one up at a time and setting them to the side. Then he got to one that had white powder on it. He closed his eyes and began chanting so fast that I couldn't make out most of the words. He held the paper above his head and said holy ash had manifested on it. A friend, who'd been into Sai Baba, told me she'd seen him manifest it out of thin air, but I'd never witnessed it before. In the Upanishads, it's called *vibhuti*. I was sure Trivedi had put it there when he'd left the room.

I hadn't told Trivedi anything about Alan and was interested to see what he'd come up with. Trivedi carefully brushed the ashes into a brass cup and set it on the altar. His eyes rolled up, and he seemed to go into a trance. He began reading the paper in Sanskrit and translating it into English. For the sake of the sanity of my dear readers and those listening to the audiobook, I'll give mostly the English translation so you can go with the flow. However, I won't edit it to make it more readable.

Trivedi looked at a complicated chart on the document for a while, then looked directly at me and asked, "Do you read Sanskrit?" I said, "I can speak some Sanskrit, but I'm not able to read it." He held the paper up for me as he pointed to a word. I could barely believe my eyes. It was one of the few words I knew in Sanskrit—my name!

Trivedi said the reading was for me, but I didn't see how that could be since I didn't have an astrology chart. Had he written it after we came in? My skepticism was still intact as he read on:

"Three foreigner ladies you see at present have come to this place. Valerie and those with you are known by names Anette and Doreen. All have many questions in their minds. Some questions now do not have any relevance. They have no use. Whatever is required for the benefit of the soul, I am only telling those things. Valerie, to know of her mother and father. The name is not useful at present." My suspicions vanished in astonishment.

Trivedi went on: "In before life she took birth in India near the Ganges River. At that time, mother delivered her before marriage and left her in Varanasi. Some other parents collected her and brought her up. Now, in this birth, they again became her parents. This is most unusual that she got a similar fate as her previous birth."

I flashed on seeing an abandoned infant on the street in Delhi with a dog licking her ear. That sight spurred me to do a lot of work with orphans in India.

Trivedi continued, "At the present moment for the benefit of her soul, I tell her that she repeats the mantra *Aum Nama Shivaya* 11 times 100,000 times with a rudraksha mala. She may do this over the next four years. In order to wipe out previous karmas known and unknown, she also may recite to Shiva."

How could Trivedi know my personal mantra? I had already been using the rudraksha mala Ram Dev gave me, using the exact same mantra that Gurudev gave me.

Trivedi continued: "One *yagna* fire ceremony should also be performed in three parts. She has smooth spiritual life. Some karmas done in previous birth gets fruit accordingly. Good karma is born in this her worldly life. Watch your guru and suddenly something will happen when you are far away. If your faith is kept in your guru, then you have no problem getting liberation in this life. You are with your guru more than ten years. You will return here in the future two times. At this moment, only this much is provided."

Skepticism Shattered

Trivedi didn't know I had a guru or anything else about me. Totally stupefied, I sat there as he went on to read some things about Alan, Anette, and Doreen. He said it took all of them being here, as well as the Sikh family, to match me astrologically to my banana leaf. There was no way Trivedi could have made all this up. The mention of my specific mantra, which only my Gurudev knew, convinced me Trivedi was not a fraud. It was all so surreal!

The old saint, who had briefly come in earlier, returned. He had a large beautiful flower mala this time and walked straight to me as I stood up. Putting the mala around my neck, he knelt on the floor, touching my feet before I knew what was happening. I pulled him up by his shoulders as a tear rolled down his thin cheek. With his hands clasped together, he asked me to walk in the garden with him for a few minutes. I wondered if the old man was in his right mind and looked to Trivedi for guidance. Trivedi said he lived at the temple, and he'd never seen him do this with anyone before. I gave my respects to Trivedi and left an envelope with an offering on the altar. My friends stayed and talked to the others while I turned to Swami.

Out in the sunlit courtyard, we slowly walked in silence. Swami spoke little English, but I understood his Punjabi-accented Hindi when he said I needed to go to Haridwar. He said I should do mantras standing in the Ganges River. Then he told me he recognized me from a previous life.

I asked if he had been my father in Varanasi. Swami reached out with his frail wrinkled hands and took mine to his chest. He said, "My dear one, I am very happy to see you again."

My friends came out, and Swami bowed to them and opened the gate for us to leave. I assured him as I parted that I took his words to heart and was going to Haridwar soon.

I don't think I'd believe it if there had not been witnesses and audio recordings of the experience. Anette, Doreen, and I were beyond awestruck as we traveled back to Delhi for them to catch flights home. I returned to Haridwar with a bounty of fruits and nuts for Gurudev and shared what had happened the best I could. He simply smiled as usual when something miraculous had occurred.

I walked down to the *Mata Ganga* river with flowers, and the rudraksha mala Baba Ram Dev had given me after the Kumbha Mela. Wading into her waters, casting rose petals, and reciting my mantra became an ongoing practice. I made it easy by learning numerous Shiva bhajans and devotional songs, and I made up a few more of my own using the many names of Shiva. I figured I'd easily sing Aum Namah Shivaya a thousand times a week and eventually fulfill the Brighu suggestion. That way, I wouldn't have to count out 100,000 to the 11th power. That worked great until the Indian government meddled in my plans.

"The truth will set you free. But not until it is finished with you."
- David Foster Wallace

19

THE LIVING LANGUAGE

I asked Gurudev again about giving him my assets. I thought
the most powerful thing I could do was to support him.
What he'd given me was priceless, and I wanted to contribute
to his work. He again said that wasn't needed and I could
manage those assets better than anyone else. Then he added,
"Ask me again in seven years." I thought this was odd and
often wondered what might change in seven years.

About six years later, the Indian government changed its
visa requirements. The new law was that an American citizen
had to leave the country after 180 days for two months. It
was wintertime, and that's when we were always in India.
When my visa was up, I had to leave. Heavy-hearted to be
oceans away from him, I was in shock integrating back into
an unfamiliar American life.

Soon after I left, my Gurudev experienced a brain
hemorrhage. All my calls and emails remained unanswered.
I imagined his new aides were trying to keep this from
becoming public knowledge. My hands were tied, and there

was nothing I could do to help. I sent flowers and letters addressed to him but got no response.

The long separation from Gurudev was excruciating. With no contact, I felt betrayed by my extended Indian family. Issues of abandonment consumed me. I tried to remember to be detached, but it didn't help.

Restless anxiety made picking up the pieces of the life I'd left behind challenging. Mindlessly I swept, scrubbed, mopped, polished, and purged the house of things I didn't need to make it feel more like an ashram. Days turned into weeks, and my calls and emails went unanswered. The heaviness in my heart ached to have some contact with Gurudev. I felt an emptiness I'd only experienced once before in my life. That's when my dad Julius passed away.

Déjà vu

I began to organize and type up handwritten notes I'd made in India. Then I turned to transcribe CDs I'd made. Sorting through a pile of them to decide where to start, I had an uncanny feeling that I'd already gone through them. Everything around me was like a déjà vu. I had been sitting in this same chair in my dining room, with my computer in front of me and my right hand on this exact spread of CDs on the table. Had I dreamt it? Was it a premonition? Another possibility was that I had rehearsed this part of my life before.

The CD my hand had rested upon was the Brighu readings. I remembered Trivedi's words, "Watch your guru, and suddenly something will happen when you are far away." That was assuredly referring to the stroke Gurudev just had. I listened to the entire session with headphones, typing the key points as fast as possible.

Picking up my mala from the altar, I did dozens of rounds of chanting Aum Namah Shivaya. For the next three nights, I lit a ceremonial fire feeding it ghee and herbs to complete the three Yagna rituals recommended in the Brighu reading. I repeatedly played my Aum Namah Shivaya CDs and carried them in my car to chant with when I drove anywhere.

Return to India

I flew back to Gurudev at the end of my exile. Arriving in Delhi, I learned he was recovering in Bangalore at Swami Vivekananda's Holistic Center. I caught the next flight and was picked up by the center's welcoming team that night. They accommodated me in a room a few minutes from the house where Gurudev was staying.

At daybreak, I went to his house, and Gurudev's new assistant informed me I could only see him at specific times. He was in charge now and didn't want my help. I had to be okay with that, but it was soul-crushing. I sat outside the house and began softly singing Aum Namah Shivaya. Gurudev heard me, and soon the door opened. I was able to see him privately, and all the torment of our long separation faded. He was in good spirits and was going to be all right.

He didn't know I was coming and hadn't gotten any of my messages. After his stroke, the new assistant handled all his communications. Gurudev said he'd take his phone back if my messages weren't getting through to him. He'd never even received the flower deliveries I'd sent. I read him some emails I'd sent to those close to him. His eyebrows drew together as he asked me to read them all. The last thing I wanted to do was upset him, but he asked me to, so I did. Afterward, I assured him everything was okay now that I knew he was recovering well. His benevolent gaze into my eyes was a treasure I tucked into my heart.

I wondered if he had a premonition before the stroke and asked him. He looked down and arranged books on his bed. I knew this was a sign of disinterest in the subject. I reminded him he told me to ask him again in seven years about giving my assets to him. This was the seventh year, and I offered everything to him again. With a gentle, loving smile, he said, "*Nahi*," which is the polite word in Sanskrit for no. I loved this man with all my heart and soul. The trust and bonding that developed between us was the most precious asset of my life.

I played part of the Brighu recording from my phone, as he'd never heard the part that said something would happen to him while I was far away. Gurudev's new assistant came in and said it was time for breakfast and that my time was up. Gurudev asked him to have chai prepared for me. We laughed after he left, and Gurudev said that many humans are susceptible to catching the disease of jealousy. I told him I must have caught the disease of attachment because I'd missed him so much. My eyes welled up, but this time it was an eruption of sheer joy to be in his presence again.

Gurudev gave me his schedule for Ayurvedic treatments and invited me to go with him on his daily walks. When chai and breakfast arrived, Gurudev asked his assistant to inform me whenever spontaneous satsangs happened. One of Gurudev's caregivers came in and was kind enough to tell me the kinds of treatments Gurudev was having. I told him I'd love to get Ayurvedic training, and he said he'd arrange it.

Over the next six months, I spent every possible minute with Gurudev.

After his daily walk, he began giving satsangs every day to the groups of devotees that came to visit, as well as many students on campus. It was a vast Ayurvedic center and college. Many foreigners were taking classes, and Gurudev encouraged me to do the same. I carefully mapped out times I couldn't be with him and got into Sanskrit and Ayurvedic programs. Beyond that, I found a sewing machine, whipped up a unique garment for Gurudev to wear in healing sessions, and wrote new songs to sing at the satsangs.

It was a period of going deeper into Gurudev's teachings. There were savvy Sanskrit translators around that guided me beyond what my language skills had previously allowed. I recorded every session, noting paramount statements in my journal.

As my six-month visa approached expiration, I knew that my position as Gurudev's assistant was history. I talked to Gurudev about how I could be supportive after leaving India. My idea was to convert all his old satsang videos and tapes to digital media. I wanted everything uploaded for his teachings to be widely available. He was pleased and supportive of the project.

Flying back and forth between visa exiles didn't look good. I wasn't his ongoing assistant anymore, and flights had doubled in price since my first arrival. Plus, the use of fossil fuels was disturbing. I'd already been planting hundreds of trees in India with Gurudev to offset our carbon footprint of travels around the world. If I flew round trip every six months, that'd add up to about 68,000 air miles. I'd need to plant about 16 trees a month to balance it out, not counting other transportation.

On my last day with Gurudev, he told me I was needed in America. He said people would come to me with matters I have knowledge about. He didn't say what that might look like.

He popped me lovingly on the head, giving me his blessings to leave. I didn't know when I'd see my beloved spiritual father again.

Fire of Separation

Back in Asheville, I took care of things at the ecovillage and worked on getting Gurudev's teachings up online. A fire of separation burned within me, and nothing I did extinguished the flame. I still wasn't beyond attachments and wanted to return to Gurudev. I paid it forward on my carbon credits by sending family and friends holiday gifts of trees planted in their names.

When my time of banishment was up, I returned. The long 22-hour flight and 11-hour time change always did me in for a day, but I didn't want to waste any precious time. I felt most at home when I was by his side. The depth of our connection was like nothing I had ever experienced before. Some people said we had been together in many previous lives, but I had no memory of that. All I knew was that the living language was alive when I was in his presence. Since my first encounter with Gurudev in Asheville, a continual state of synchronicity has guided me to trust the unexplainable.

When I landed in Delhi, I discovered Gurudev was in *Mawie Dham*, a small rural village on the banks of the Yamuna River where he was born. It was in the state of Uttar Pradesh, over 300 miles away. I caught a train, and before I fell asleep, I asked the conductor to wake me before our arrival.

Gurudev has 14 ashrams around India, and this was one of my favorites. He'd opened the first women's college in the region, and foreign donations bought the first school bus and ambulance. The ashram was so far out that the usual hoards of devotees flocking to see him wouldn't come. Only a few vehicles traversed the narrow bullock-cart road leading to the village. It was always a reprieve from the honking chaos of the cities.

After a 12-hour stop-and-go ride, Gurudev's driver met me on the platform in the wee hours of the morning. He caught me up on the last six months on the two-hour drive to the ashram. The best news was that Gurudev was fully recovered. Speeding down the dark, bumpy one-lane dirt road, I sang in Sanskrit: *"Twameva Mata cha Pita Twameva ...."* The song meant, "You are my mother and father, my true family and friend." This song's also on my Nectar of Grace album that Gurudev had me record.

I got to a room in the ashram and popped open my bulging bag, spilling out bags of heirloom seeds and dozens of solar lights that were snuggled into socks. The ashram had little power but was rich in having over 100 acres of agricultural land. I'd soon be getting my hands in the dirt with Gurudev.

At daybreak, I found him sitting outside the temple devotees had built at his birthplace. When our eyes met, I didn't need to say anything. He poured his chai into a glass, handed it to me, and ordered more. He always had me served two chai teas because he'd seen the enormous mugs in America.

On our morning walk through the gardens, we heard a cow bellowing and went to the cow house, the *goshala*, and watched a birthing. Within a few minutes, the calf was wobbling on her feet, and mom was licking her sweet face. I kept turning away, not because of seeing blood, but because witnessing the birth and bonding triggered a dark hidden wound needing healing. I don't know what I went through as an infant when taken from my mother, but watching the scene brought some primal feelings to light. Looking at Gurudev for reassurance, he said, "Every day is a new day. We'll name the baby calf *Suryaday,* meaning sunrise."

The morning dew rose like steam as we walked over to see a devotee shoveling cow dung into the composting gas digester. The kitchen once had an open fire but now had plenty of gas to cook with. The breakfast bell rang, and we returned to Gurudev's outdoor lounge chair. I always ate after him, and this day he scooted part of his meal onto another plate and handed it to me. That was prasad. Afterward, a casual satsang was in the courtyard, where I set out all the solar lights. For the next two days, Gurudev and I planted seeds.

When we left Mawie Dham, we traveled to several large satsangs and many of his other ashrams. I was able to be by his side every day. Back when I had been singing for enormous crowds, Gurudev asked me to give short satsangs along with my songs. I had a repertoire of different topics and began sharing those again.

The months were filled with singing, satsangs, and spontaneous projects wherever we went. Even though I was busy, I didn't feel as useful as when I was his assistant. Gurudev said to relax and enjoy my time. Relaxing had never been something I was good at. My life glorified busyness. I always had to be doing something. Maybe because I always thought I owed my life to my parents and had the habit of trying to show my worth.

I did back off on some projects and focused more on *bhakti* yoga. Gurudev had told me years before that my path was through sound, and I'd use my voice in my yogic practice. Singing was in my soul and led me to Bhakti yoga. In America, when someone talks about yoga, most people think of physical postures. Once at a New York university, Gurudev was addressing professors and students about yoga. The hall was filled with people sitting on yoga mats when we arrived. He told them that physical postures can be a beginning method but that he was there to explain the four yogic paths of *Karm, Gyan, Bhakti,* and *Raja.* In the end, he did one yoga posture to appease them: lifting his entire body off the ground at an angle with one hand supporting him.

With Gurudev's guidance, I dabbled in all the paths but wasn't disciplined in any. Bhakti yoga was my primary practice; singing and dancing seemed natural to me from the time I could walk and talk. Sometimes when I sang, it was like something else was coming through me. The same happened when I danced, especially ecstatic dance. Gurudev said that because I was into seva, I was also a Karm yogi— or *yogini* to be exact- a female yogi. He said I exemplified that in our campaign to ban plastic bags. One on this path is fearless, and he said I had to be fearless to live in India for so many years.

The six-month mark was closing in on me. After many road trips, train rides, and flights, we ended up in his Haridwar ashram for my last week. His daily satsangs, which sometimes happened as many as four times a day now, always revealed something new. This week, he keyed in on what renunciation meant. He didn't mince words when speaking to a few sanyasis. They're called saints in India, but I'd met many sanctimonious types. Gurudev said, "It's not giving up things that matter as much as giving up the unhealthy pride of the ego. It's not about wearing orange robes and prayer beads or standing on your head. Renunciation comes from glorification inside. Outward glorification is the remnants of ego."

I was astonished by the chutzpah display of some sannyasis, especially the men. Some complained that I didn't touch their feet. Once, a young *Sadhvi,* a female saint, told Gurudev that I'd put in fake eyes and my blue ones weren't real. She questioned him about how I could be a renunciant since I was so vain. Gurudev called me to sit with them and gave a satsang about jealousy. I listened without realizing the context of the talk. Ultimately, he said, "Valerie doesn't even know how to be jealous." It was only afterward that I found out what had prompted his satsang.

Many times, I'd experienced animosity behind Gurudev's back. Some saints and devotees didn't like that I'd become his assistant. I could understand, as I might have reacted the same way in their shoes. One devotee with him for over 30 years instigated a power struggle with me. At Gurudev's insistence, we developed a long-term friendship. I used my duck medicine technique: shaking off the animosity that splashed on me and letting it roll off.

Gurudev said I was a true devotee. If that was so, then why wasn't I disciplined? My meditation and yoga practices certainly weren't structured. Dancing yoga, chanting, and singing didn't require any disciplined effort. After a decade, no matter how much I tried to please my spiritual father, I still couldn't sit in a lotus position for half an hour. What I did do was follow the living language and get out of my own way.

Unusual Challenges

I continually strove to accept whatever conditions I found myself in. Living in an Indian environment required a lot of adjustments. We moved around so much that some weeks I'd sleep in a different bed every night.

One of the first oddities I encountered was trying to go to the bathroom in Indian toilets. Not only did I have to squat my unyogic body down close to the floor where the toilet was, but many times the water was on the right side, and I was only supposed to use my left hand to wash my private parts. How in the world did they do that? I gave up wearing underwear early in the game as it always seemed to get wet when I attempted the acrobatics I had to perform. I then took to wearing long robes, which made things easier—plus, the airflow was welcome in the intense heat.

The heat waves were unbearable. At one point, my nose began to bleed profusely. Gurudev acted as my loving father, and he took me in for tests. The doctors said the cause was that the heat was too much for me. They said nose bleeds also happen to babies as they get used to the intense climate. The bloody experience was worth it to feel the fatherly care my teacher bestowed upon me.

Other challenges included the feat of washing my clothes. I didn't want others to do it for me, as I'd seen how they lay clothes on the cement and then take a rock and scrub them. My clothes would be in tatters in no time doing it that way. I came up with my own method. There always was a bucket in the showers, and I'd ask for a second one. I put some clothes in each bucket, added soap and water, then put one foot in each and jumped back and forth, agitating them like a washing machine. Then I'd do the same with fresh water to rinse them. It worked great, plus my feet got spanking clean. If I had two buckets, it was a five-star ashram to me.

When I first wore white in India, I'd hang my wet clothes on a line with clothespins. Many saints simply draped theirs over a bush or laid them out on the ground, but inevitably some saint would hang his next to mine, double clipping them together. I'd find my whites partially orange from the dye that bled onto them, and no amount of washing helped. Also, my clothespins would disappear, and I'd find my clothes blown off.

Besides that, monkeys loved pulling down clothes and prancing around with them. I began carrying around a clothesline and hanging mine in my room under a fan. Whenever someone I knew came to India, I'd ask them to bring more clothespins. Pretty soon, I was able to leave clothespins everywhere I went.

I also had to learn how to press clothes since most of mine were linen and scrunched up terribly in my bag. Where was my mother when I needed her? Why had I never learned these skills? People always had irons in their homes and at the ashrams, but the electrical outlets were never close enough to plug into. So, I developed the fine art of wall ironing. I'd string ropes up in any way possible that allowed me to hang clothes next to the outlet. Then I'd hold one part of the garment up to the wall with my right knee, stretch the fabric out with my left hand, grab the hot iron in my right hand, and press away. It was quite an achievement.

After my first year of lugging around luggage, I learned to travel with one small bag to meet my basic needs. I traded in my sheets for a shawl, my pillow for a towel, and my brush for my fingers. Continually, I reminded myself that I was not there for comfort. It was a mantra of sorts.

Another thing I wrangled with was refusing third servings of food. Because I was with Gurudev, I ate the same food they prepared for him. It made them so happy that I'd eat seconds and tell them how wonderful it was. They felt privileged to cook for Gurudev, and I didn't want to hurt their feelings. I gained a substantial amount of weight without realizing it. Now, where's the discipline in that?

Despite the challenges of living in India and losing creature comforts, I thrived under Gurudev's wings. Satsangs in Haridwar continued to focus on the renunciation theme. The more he explained, the more I pondered my abstention. The living language was speaking to me from all directions, urging me to look closer at the part I was playing. I didn't feel like I'd given up anything except comfort.

On the contrary, an avalanche of incredible experiences enriched me every day. I really was not a renunciant. The protocols that went along with being a Sadhvi felt presumptuous. Toe touching and acknowledgments were what most of the sanyasi thrived on. Instead of wearing the standard saintly orange colors, I took to dressing on the edge of the sunset spectrum in reds. That felt better than parading about looking like all the other saints. I could play the part when need be, but to fill the role, I had to get into it.

20

DEEP SELFOLOGY

What could I give up beyond comfort? The only thing that came to mind was my attachment to Gurudev. Lifetimes of lessons from my spiritual father over the past decade had changed me. He'd taught me how to be my own mother and father. In his presence, I knew what it meant to feel safe.

There was a fullness in me, and I wondered if my work in India was complete. Was I at the finale of an eleven-year cycle in my life? The living language showed me an era was ending, and it was time for my next step. I'd never heard of anyone doing what I was thinking about, but I went for it. A few days before leaving, I renounced renunciation.

I got enough black fabric to make a long Sadhvi gown and a large scarf to wrap over my head. I stitched it up in my room using one of my outfits as a pattern. The challenging part was feeding the fabric into the machine with my left hand while spinning the wheel with my right hand to make it go.

I wrote a presentation for the announcement. I needed it to be loving and acceptable. Once satisfied with my speech, I was ready to present it in costume the next morning.

Just after daybreak, I peeked out my window, observing a bunch of saints and devotees already gathered outside Gurudev's door, waiting for him to appear. He always came out in the morning to have chai on the couch bed outside his room before giving a spontaneous talk based on whatever someone asked.

After Gurudev was seated with chai in hand, I walked out. As I approached, someone turned and pointed at me. Numerous heads spun to see what was going on. Gurudev looked up as I walked through the group and sat silently beside him. His eyes took me in from top to bottom and then looked me in the eye. Everyone was waiting for an explanation.

I spoke to the group first. "I've taken all of Gurudev's recent satsangs on renunciation to heart. Sainthood is indeed dangerous to one's ego because sannyasis are treated with such high respect. Sometimes, this leads to self-pride and arrogance. The temptation to allow others to think sannyasis are superior is obvious. For the past week, I've contemplated what the greatest renunciation might be." Then turning to Gurudev, I bowed my head and said, "I am renouncing renunciation."

He knew I wasn't kidding. Gurudev looked around at the devotees and began another satsang on the renunciation theme. He mentioned all the things I'd given up. Life in a comfortable country, food I was used to, coffee I loved, friends, and an ecovillage I'd left behind. He said I'd served him as a real devotee, not just with words but by deeds. He used me as an example to teach what a true devotee is. I'd offered him everything with my time, skills, and possessions.

I learned Hindi because I wanted to know what he was saying. He asked how many Hindi-speaking devotees still needed clarification to understand him. How many only came on specific holy days? How many saints would handle their egos in such a way as to renounce the highly respected status of being a saint?

Silence fell over the crowd. Gurudev poured the rest of his chai into a cup and handed it to me, sporting an affectionate smile. He then whacked his hand on my crown chakra. He had blessed my renunciation.

Leaving my Spiritual Father

When I left India again, Gurudev told me I'd be teaching in America. Me, teaching? I asked him what that looked like. He said it would be shown to me and I didn't have to go looking for it. He advised, however, that I needed to smooth someone's arm before injecting teachings. It was a private joke, but I knew what he meant.

Gurudev said that helping in America would be easier since English was my mother tongue. He congratulated me on learning Hindi and said it would continue to be helpful. He laughed about how Indians were shocked at some things I'd say in Hindi. One example was my pronunciation of *kainchi*, the Hindi word for scissors. I always had a tool card with scissors to open letters and packages for him. I lost them often and would ask if anyone had seen my scissors. For over a year, I didn't understand why Gurudev laughed at me about that. I was so embarrassed when he finally explained that I used a similar word that meant panties when I pronounced it. I'd been asking if anyone had seen my panties!

No wonder people thought I was being irreverent. How could I speak to their Krishna, their God, in such a casual way? But why didn't they tell me about my goof-ups? I never thought I was being disrespectful. I guess it was a cosmic setup to make a fool of myself. Because Gurudev had always laughed when I bungled up, I was his entertainment channel.

Gurudev had become my family, my mother, father, and best friend. Being removed from his presence again wouldn't be easy. In India, saying goodbye or asking where someone is going is bad luck. I departed from the Haridwar ashram, lost in a decade of memories.

The Ring

America was a culture shock. Everything was too big, too much, and too privileged. If I glimpsed at a television, it was like watching a Saturday Night Live episode. Even listening to Democracy Now and public radio was surreal. Conversations were hard to engage in, as most of the time, the subjects didn't interest me.

Rereading a book on Gurudev's teachings I'd published called 108 Insights was comforting. It was as if he were speaking to me for the first time. "Perform the scenes of your life like an actress who never forgets her true identity. Although the costumes and scenes of your life will change, you yourself are changeless."

My costume and scene had radically changed, but I didn't know what role I was operating in. I'd rented out my home at Earthaven Ecovillage for the rest of the year and needed a new home. I moved to Green Oaks Community, a six-acre tract with five homes that our initial founding group secured before buying the large tract of Earthaven land.

The property had deteriorated badly, so I spent months in overalls playing a construction role. The main house, built in 1927, was in terrible shape. I absorbed myself in repairs with little time for anything else. When it came to the finishing touches, I draped saris on the windows and soon created a sparkling clean sanctuary embracing me in the colors of the sunset. Next, I started a large garden and herb beds. Having my hands in the dirt grounded me. I fell in love with the land, and my new home, but something was still off.

People I hardly knew came to me asking for guidance about one thing or another, but I wasn't sure how to help them. The more I knew, the less I knew. Gurudev instilled in me that we are our own Guru, which is what I attempted to lead people to. Although I still ask the Almighty for guidance, I know my Soul, my higher Self, gives the answers. One of the most significant gifts I received during my 11 years in India was learning how to trust. To trust me first. That's all I could guide people to do—to learn to trust themselves.

I was different from the person who left for India over a decade ago. I'd learned a lot but wanted to go deeper into self-inquiry. Did I really know who I was? I was clear that I'm a soul and will never die, but what about me as an everyday character? To help me answer that question, I turned back to writing. I began daily journaling, and many more memories of my time with Gurudev flowed forth.

The extensive traveling with Gurudev enriched my life in ways I didn't even realize. I got a world map and sketched the zigzagged flight patterns we had taken over the past decade. Looking at it, I remembered a psychic in Cassadaga I'd had a reading with years before. Her premonition was that I'd meet a foreigner visiting America who'd be important in my life. She said I'd travel with him across the oceans in a triangle pattern at least seven times. The sketched lines I made on the map had nine different triangles showing the flights we had taken!

Searching through numerous old cassette tapes of psychics I'd consulted, I found that recording and listened to it again. Initially, I thought the man she referred to might be my natural father coming to look for me or perhaps a future partner. She said I'd recognize the foreigner by his ring. She had sketched the ring's design in my journal so I'd identify him. Digging through old journals, I found the drawing. I'd never made the connection before. It clearly depicted one of the two rings Gurudev gave me that I was wearing on my hand!

A devotee gave Gurudev two rings in England: a gold man's ring with an unusual symbol and a women's platinum diamond ring. When packing things to leave, I told him the rings were precious and not to misplace them. He picked up the gold ring and held it out to me saying, "I have no use for this, you want?" Despite his notoriety, he was humble and generous. With a bit of reluctance to accept such an expensive gift, I took it as his prasad and slid it on my left index finger.

Then he held out the second ring. The diamond embedded in it was exquisite, and I told him that selling it could support his work. Looking closely at the ring, he twirled it around and then held it out to me again. Looking up into his eyes, a deep feeling of connection erupted into a flow of tears spilling down my cheeks. Composing myself, I said I was touched by the offer but that it was too small for my big fingers. I raised my hands, wiggling my long wide fingers above my head. He reached over, took my right hand, and slid it on my ring finger. That moment remains frozen in time for me.

I'd been so focused on discovering my birth mother's name in Cassadaga that nothing else seemed important. Now here I was, years later, finding out that much of what the psychic said had come true. It blew me away looking at my rings and all the triangular lines on the map connecting Delhi, the USA, Peru, England, Brazil, Singapore, New Zealand, Dubai, and Europe.

Two psychics from that time also told me I'd be writing a book. I began writing about the ring connection, and the more I wrote, the more I understood how experiences with Gurudev tied into my adoption. I've been writing ever since.

For years I called myself an ontologist and figured that the study of beingness applies to us all, right? Writing turned me on to studying myself in a new way. I decided my new role was that of a selfologist. I looked it up in the dictionary and was surprised to find out it's not a word, and there are no origins for it. Well, I didn't know where I came from, so that suited me fine. I called my writing practice "Deep Selfology."

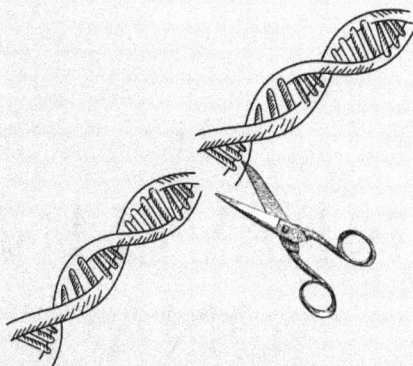

PART 4
MISSING
LINKS

21

UNRAVELING DNA

My friend Barnes came and dowsed my place for a well. He asked how Earthaven was doing as he had been involved in the early years. I told him I felt complete and was going to let that part of my life go. I didn't feel a calling to go back. I was happy in my new home and wanted to try out a sustainable lifestyle in town. Leaving Earthaven, after the enormous time and energy that I had given to the vision, was like seeing my child go off to college. Or maybe it was like the kids wanted to throw a scolding mother out of the house. Or maybe it was a subconscious 'abandon before you can be abandoned' thinking that turned me around. Some felt I had abandoned Earthaven when I left for India. In some ways I did. Whatever it was, I knew I was done.

Searching for my biological family is what I was hot on. Barnes said he'd taken the National Geographic Geno test and discovered so much about his ancestors he hadn't known. He urged me to get my DNA tested.

It took a while for me to act on that but in the summer of 2015, I got a test kit. When the results came in, I was disappointed to find no matches. But what I did find out added even more mystery to my search. My results showed I have one of the world's highest percentages of Denisovan DNA. Denisovan? I'd never even heard about them. I googled it, and what appeared was ... "Meet the strangest hybrid in human history."

Denisovans

The Denisovans were only discovered in 2010, and no one I asked had heard about them. Russian scientists found a finger bone and tooth in a cave in Siberia dated about 40,000 years old. Denisovans were an ancient race thought to have been around as early as 500,000 years ago. Archeologists also found a beautiful bracelet made from green cut stone that was polished and precisely drilled. No one seemed to know much about these beings who were different from Neanderthals. But one tidbit I found reported that Denisovans had long fingers. My adoptive mom had told everyone that the first thing she noticed about me was my long fingers. The information rocked my boat. My roots were from a totally different Homo genus, classified as a new species of archaic humans! Not only did I not know who my birth family was, but even if I did, it seemed not even DNA could tell me who my ancestors were.

I reflected again on ancient Vedic texts that mention flying chariots and machines called *Virmanas*. Was our planet seeded with interstellar life? I wondered how those texts related to later biblical references in Genesis of angels coming to the Earth and mating with the beautiful women. Were the Denisovans the "Nephilim" referred to in the biblical texts? For a quick reference, look at Genesis 6:4 where it's written, "The Nephilim were on the Earth in those days when the sons of God would sleep with the daughters of humankind, who gave birth to their children. They were the mighty heroes of old, the famous men." Who were these heroes, and why were they famous? Did ancient gods and fallen angels come by flying machines and mate with Neanderthals? And were their offspring now called Denisovans? I felt more alien than ever.

One positive thing I learned is that interbreeding with the Denisovans gave humans an immune system upgrade, making them more disease resistant. Some believe that humans needed the archaic DNA to survive.

I wondered if the Denisovans had O-negative blood and if they became extinct because of mating with other human blood types. Since O-negatives mating outside their blood type causes hemolytic diseases that can be lethal for a fetus, it seemed like a logical conclusion in my unscientific mind. Only about seven percent of the population today has O-negative blood. Scientists haven't succeeded in reproducing it, and they still don't know where it originated. Did we lose all previous knowledge about our ancestors when the Earth flooded? Did the myths that evolved point to the truth of the remnants of ancient civilizations? Maybe the O-negatives were genetic work done by a previous advanced civilization.

I wondered how many of the adoptees I'd connected with years ago also had Denisovan DNA. Were we a sought after strange breed in the hidden black market baby arrangements in the fifties? Were we experimental beings that were being tracked? Some O-negatives believe that's true.

Exhausting all the information I found on the internet, I climbed back out of the rabbit hole. With my high amount of Denisovan DNA, I imagined the good thing was that I might have many more decades to unravel the mysteries of my origins.

First Match

Solid answers to the avalanche of mysteries mounted. The enigma of Denisovan and O-negative blood research kept me mind-flossing for over a year. I turned my focus to homing in on my birth mother again.

A friend told me to test with a company called Ancestry because the results would tell me the names of others who tested that matched my DNA. Just before the Winter Solstice in 2016, I got my second testing kit and sent it off. My understanding was that if I got at least a first cousin match, I could unravel my DNA and discover my heritage.

The results came in with hundreds of matches but no first cousins. The closest match was a possible second, but it only showed their initials since the person was still living. I'm against printing things out on paper if it's available digitally, but the mass of information was too overwhelming to comprehend on my computer screen. I bought a printer, a ream of recycled paper, sticky notes, colored highlighters, paste and tape, and dove in.

I printed out my matches and any family trees they'd created. Then I matched up the trees as best as possible. I cut and pasted until my enormous oak work table overflowed with a paper patchwork that draped off onto the floor. Soon the paper tree branches made their way through my kitchen and into the dining room. The project was so big that I couldn't reach the edges to add more without stepping on it. When my friend Steve Torma came over, he had to play hopscotch over the small open areas on the floor to get to me. Seeing my kerfuffle, he had an idea to organize my mess.

Steve lived next door and returned with four by five feet banners used in his workshops. He'd sprayed them with something tacky that the papers adhered to. As I discovered new elements, I'd pull pieces off and re-stick them on my elaborate puzzle. The banners were different colors, so I attempted to separate my maternal and paternal. They hung all around my workroom, leaving a small space to crawl out from to get to the kitchen. I was bug-eyed living on caffeine, bananas, and popcorn.

I spent the day getting all the clues stuck up, but making sense of it all was a mind-twister. Several political connections in my DNA had me thinking I was a descendant of Ulysses S. Grant. I sent numerous messages to those matches but had little to tell them since I didn't know my birth parent's surnames. Weeks of researching and another ream of paper later, I didn't seem any closer to knowing where I came from.

A girlfriend came by, and as she made her way into my paper trail display and looked around, she said, "I'm taking you to a movie you absolutely have to see." I was game for a break and the next showing of *The Lion* was in 15 minutes. We grabbed some snacks and scurried out.

The movie is a true story of a child named Saroo, who was lost at a train station in India. Having lived there myself for over a decade, it brought back memories of seeing dozens of raggedy children begging in the stations. Once, when getting on a train, I took off my shoes and gave them to a barefoot little girl with only one arm. She quickly grabbed them and ran off. As the train departed, I looked out, and there she was in her new oversized shoes. A big grin flashed behind her one hand waving at me as she faded into the distance. From then on, every time I took a train, I left a pair of shoes at the boarding ramp. Whenever I left the country, I'd leave all my shoes on the curb outside the airport, keeping only the pair on my feet. It was one of my top feel goods.

The story of Saroo's search and reunion with his family is powerfully portrayed and played on the emotional journey of my own search. When it came to the scene where Saroo had papers and maps taped up all over his wall, my friend elbowed me and whispered, "That's you."

I was re-inspired, and when I got home, I did my daily check on Ancestry to see if there were any new matches. Whoohoo ... I had a first cousin! There was no name, only the initials "A.K." and a symbol showing she was female. By viewing our shared matches, which is an excellent tool on Ancestry, I knew A.K. and I had 22 shared DNA matches. I rearranged my patchwork tree to link up all the second and third cousin matches we shared. I was hot on the trail of my mother.

The person listed as the administrator for A.K.'s DNA was Dawn Wing. I found numerous people with that name on Facebook. Searching each one, I looked through their lists of friends to see if any surnames matched the ones in my DNA. Bingo! There was a Dawn with a surname match with blond hair and blue eyes like me. Looking her up on people-search websites, I found her address and phone numbers.

I planned what I'd say and called the next morning. I left messages at both of Dawn's numbers and waited. She lived a 12-hour drive from me in Naples, Florida. My friend Don spent his winters there, so I called him to see if he'd play spy for me. Loving a good mystery, he jumped into my drama. He visited some places we saw on Facebook where Dawn hung out. What was I doing sitting at home? This was no time to dilly-dally.

I called Dawn again, leaving a more detailed message this time. I revealed that I was adopted and said it would be a blessing if she'd talk to me because she was my highest DNA match on Ancestry. Another friend, Elizabeth, whom I'd met in Peru, also lived in Naples. When I called and updated her on my search, she invited me to stay with her. I called Don and told him I was coming down. He informed me of some fancy places Dawn frequented and said to bring upscale clothes and not to forget classy shoes.

Canceling everything on my schedule, I hit the thrift stores and bought three stylish get-ups and red suede shoes. Once satisfied with my packing job, I hit the road before midnight and drove straight through to Naples.

Don said after I rested up from the drive, we'd go to a nightclub that Dawn frequented. I left a message for Dawn that I just happened to be in Naples for a few days and would love to talk to her. Elizabeth was into night clubbing, and after a nap we fancied up. Clicking my red heels together, we met Don at the club. We had pictures of Dawn from her Facebook site, but we found no one close to resembling her. It was a long shot, but I had to try everything that might get me closer to answers. After the evening wound down, we left, clueless.

The following day, I got a message from Dawn through Facebook saying she had gotten my messages, but she didn't know what I was talking about or who A.K. was. She said she'd dabbled with the Ancestry site once but had never had a DNA test, much less being an admin for someone. I called Ancestry to see if someone who had never taken Ancestry's DNA test could have a profile on their site. The answer was no. It left me thinking that Dawn wasn't telling the truth. It was a day of feeling rejected and hopeless. But I wasn't one to surrender to defeat.

Elizabeth let me spread out my enormous paper tree, and we jumped into detective mode. We came to the same conclusion that Dawn was my first cousin and had to be A.K.'s daughter. Maybe she was married, which is why her last name differed from A.K.'s. I visited more of Dawn's haunts, but all my snooping around proved useless. After a week, I left Naples totally bummed out. Making the long journey back to Asheville, I contemplated my sanity about all the goose chases I'd been on during my search.

Maybe I wasn't supposed to know the truth. Was it my ego that refused defeat? What right did I have to focus solely on myself when so many children in the world didn't know where they came from or even have a home? In essence, I knew who I was, so did I need to hunt down my birth mother? My inner community characters were at it again, and they scampered around squabbling while I tried to get consensus on what to do. One said I had to armor up and continue the battle of the search. Another piped up saying I was too self-focused and needed to get over it and let it go. Another said I was fighting against the rhythm of life. I was at war with myself.

Go with the Flow?

I got home and ran to the bathroom, where I found the answer. A greeting card I'd taped on the wall fell on my lap. It had a character sketch of a yogi sitting in a meditation pose saying, "Always remember, my child, only dead fish go with the flow."

The yogi was right, and I wasn't dead. So many things I'd done in life were extremely challenging, like carrying out the vision to start Earthaven and working in India for so long. The New Age saying about following the path of least resistance was a bunch of bull. I stood up and flushed all my negative thoughts down the toilet. All my inner community heard me when I said, "I'm not giving up!"

A friend came over and insisted I go to an Adoption Congress in Atlanta. Hundreds of adoptees were going, and I might get some search help. I learned about the group and began connecting with other adoptees. Some said they'd had some luck testing their DNA with a company called 23andme.

I ordered my third testing kit and set to work building another paper tree. I signed up with three other companies that allowed me to load my DNA onto their online databases; Family Tree DNA, GEDmatch, and My Heritage. They were helpful free internet tools, but each had a learning curve.

I found new DNA matches through 23andme that weren't on Ancestry. They weren't close connections, but I sent messages to all the matches that looked like second or third cousins. Keeping track of all the information was mind-boggling. I made spreadsheets categorizing matches into eight columns: the percentage of DNA matches, which company I got the match from, what shared surnames matched up, any social media and contact information, whether I thought the match was my maternal or paternal side, a place to check if I had contacted them and notes on any responses I got. As the Adoption Congress drew near, I still hadn't unraveled the mystery.

Registering at the last minute, I drove to Atlanta. I jumped into all the events that specifically were about searching and reunions. No one had been on the hunt for as long as I had. Being with other adult adoptees was It was heartwarming to hear so many stories of birth-family reunions, even though some didn't have warm fuzzy endings. Everyone encouraged me to keep searching and their camaraderie was inspiring.

There were no rooms left at the hotel, but my friend found me a bed through Mary, a new friend she'd met there. Mary was from Texas and was an organizer of the event. She was also what's called a search angel that helped many adoptees connect with their birth parents. She told me, however, that she only worked with adoptees born in Texas. Every state has different laws about adoptees' rights. But Mary was an angel to me nevertheless. She let me stay with her, even though she had no idea who I was. That kind of trust opened my heart. We stayed up late talking and getting to know each other. She'd given up a child for adoption and had the most harrowing experiences of any I'd ever heard. We bonded like sisters that night. When Mary left, she told me she'd help find my family.

22

SEARCH ANGEL AID

I had a search angel on board and was ready to go full speed ahead. I asked Mary if I could call her Angel, and she said to call her anything I liked. There were so many Marys in my life, and she allowed me to dub her with the fitting title of Angel.

Catching her up on all I'd done so far, I gave her access to my DNA files. She could read all the messages I'd sent to my matches on the different sites. I made a family tree using a Hansen match I'd found on 23andme that was a possible third cousin. That was the closest I'd come to making any sense out of my adoption papers that referred to me as Infant Hanson.

For over four decades, since I first saw my Adoption Decree, I'd been looking for Hansons or any variation of that name. But for the life of me, I hadn't been able to figure out how Hansen was related to A.K. Angel explored my leads, and after a few days she told me I was way too far out on a limb to get anywhere. That wasn't the first time someone had told me I was too far out, but this time I was willing to be reeled in.

Angel had resources and connections that I didn't have access to. She told me to forget whatever I was imagining and stick with the data. She sent me prompts on what to do at each point in the process as it developed. I posted a brief of my story on a social media page called DNA Detectives. Angel volunteered with that group, and her friend Lana did as well. Lana also used her connections to help me follow the yellow brick road. Now I had two search angels watching over me!

Angel and Lana created a private family tree for me on my Ancestry account to see what that might provoke. Ancestry subscribers get hints sent to them based on family trees that people make, even if they're private. As an adoptee, I wanted to be careful not to expose too much too soon. Many times, the shame and secrecy around giving up a baby make it hard for a mother to come forward. I'd also heard rejection stories because DNA siblings thought their inheritance was at risk. I sure didn't want someone to block me out before I even got in.

My angels focused on figuring out who A.K. was. I'll refer to the surname that came up in connection with A.K. as Kavalier. I had done a rundown on all my matches to see if any of them had Kavalier in their ancestry trees. Some did, so I made another tree trying to link all of them together. It seemed logical that Kavalier was A.K.'s last name. I tried it on for size. My name is Valerie Kavalier. It had a familiar ring to it and would be a perfect pen name. I became comfortable with my new assumed name. To my surprise, my inner community all rallied around it.

Within days, my train was on track, speeding into the known. The Kavalier trees I made were a mess, but my angels repositioned things to make sense. That brought forth even more hints from Ancestry, and things fell into place. I thought I was looking for my mother, but it looked like I'd found my birth father!

His name was Henson Kavalier. I wondered if he'd used a misspelling of his first name, changing it from Henson to Hanson, when giving his name to the caseworker for my adoption. Unbelievable, but back then they might not have even checked a person's identification when filling out such an important legal document as a birth certificate. Did he intentionally give a variation of his first name, listing it as his surname? If I caught this guy, I would play some serious tricks on him. He deserved at least some intense practical jokes. I'd searched for my birth parents for decades under the surname Hanson.

He'd been married four times. Assuming he was a risque Casanova type, my inner community was all over it. "Creep, low-down lying bastard, sleazy self-centered jerk!" they screamed in my head, and on and on. The more compassionate part of myself piped up. "Maybe he had a hard time bonding in relationships, like you." But the truth was, I didn't really know Henson was my father.

My angels kept steering me back in the right direction. There was a census record of him having a daughter. The excitement of thinking I had a sister was beyond words. I searched high and low for proof that she could be my sibling. If I was on the right track, she was two years older than me. How could that be? It sank in that he must have kept her and given me away. A volcano in my heart quaked as tears spilled out like burning lava.

During my emotional landslide, Angel texted me, lifting me from my devastated state. She said A.K. was my first cousin, maybe closer, and we were on my mother's trail, not my father's. Trying to catch hold of the spinning pieces of the puzzle made me woozy. If A.K. was my first cousin on my maternal side, wouldn't she have to be the daughter of my mother's brother or sister? And who was Dawn Wing? I knew from my DNA tests that Dawn and I had no shared genealogy matches, so A.K. wouldn't be her mother. Angel texted with another message as if she were reading my mind. "You were looking at the wrong Dawn. You may be going to California soon."

Hints were whirling in as fast as the leaves falling from the oak trees above my deck. The winds shifted, shuffling the leads around until we concluded that Henson was my uncle. The daughter I'd seen on the census turned out to be only his first. With that many wives, who knew how many children he had? We found a second daughter who was about a year older than me. I'll call her Macy. Angel sent me information she found by running searches on her. It floored me to discover Macy and I went to the same high school! She was on social media sites, and I finally got the nerve to send her a message via Facebook: "Hi ... We were in high school together and are related. I'd love to talk to you." I sent her my contact information and waited.

Angel and I texted back and forth as we scoped out people that matched up with Macy on her social profile. A young man named Parker had built a family tree on Ancestry, and somehow we were connected. I'd previously sent him messages through Ancestry, asking him how we were related. His surname still made no sense to me. Macy was his friend on his social media page. They all lived in Florida, and it looked like they were my biological family. Zooming in on the photos, it became clear by the comments just who was who. Piecing it together, I was able to confirm that Parker was Macy's grandson. I sent him another message asking if

Henson Kavalier was his grandfather. It was all happening so fast.

Pressing the pause button, I unglued my eyes from the computer and looked out the window. It was snowing in October. For days, I'd paid little attention to anything besides my search and had no idea this was coming. I bundled up and gathered an armful of firewood. I lit the first fire of the season and moved my computer operations in front of the fireplace—a great way to celebrate all the mind-boggling nuggets I'd found. Once the fire was roaring, I cozied up in my lazy-girl chair. A message from Angel popped up in bold on my computer.

"Marilyn A. Kavalier," and in bigger letters under it said, "This is your mother!"

The omega moment intensified with a loud boom as sparks shot out of the fireplace. I quickly closed the glass door, laptop in hand, and looked at Angel's message again. Yes, she really was telling me she knew who my mother was. I zoomed in on her message until it filled my entire computer screen with "Marilyn A. Kavalier. This is your mother!"

Is My Mother Alive?

Angel said she didn't know whether my mother had ever been married and wasn't sure she was still alive. There are hundreds of undertakers and funeral chapels in the L.A. area, where she was supposedly from, and I began calling them. I also solicited Robert, a friend who lived in L.A., to search for me. A piece of rice on the beach would have been easier to find than my birth mother. But knowing I was closing in on her fueled my quest.

Seeing that I was running around in circles, Angel reached out to a private investigator, who ran a scan on my birth mother's name. Even he didn't find any information about marriages, possible siblings, or a death record. That meant she could still be alive. Angel said the DNA data trail would eventually lead us to her, but my birth father was even more elusive. There was nothing that made sense about him in my DNA results. I hoped I'd find my mother alive, and she'd tell me who he was.

We discovered that Henson Kavalier was my mother's brother. Nothing seemed absolute in my search, but the answers were as close as our keyboards. Henson was married once before I was born and twice afterward. He passed away in California in 2000. That was sad news to find an uncle and lose him the same day. But maybe he knew about me and told one wife or another. I ran searches on each wife, hoping to communicate with them, or at least with one. Some of my inner community still wondered if I was his daughter instead of a niece.

There were mazes within mazes of possibilities. All Kavalier's wives had changed their names, and some aliases were involved to boot. I sorted out that his first wife had five different surnames over her lifetime. I sent messages to all my DNA matches online that had any of Henson's wives' maiden names on their trees. Angel gave me access to her search resources, and I ran down oodles of phone numbers. I began calling them, and one after another found the numbers disconnected. I ran down numerous addresses and discovered everyone was in California or Florida.

The A.K. mystery escalated. It looked like Macy was Henson's daughter. DNA matches for adoptees can be deceiving. When someone's listed as a second cousin, they might be your first, but only a half-first. If they are your first cousin, they can be even closer, like a half-sister. It's a complicated unraveling. Just when you think you've got a piece of the puzzle figured out, the playing ground shifts.

Dawn was turning out to be A.K.'s daughter-in-law, which explained why she didn't share any DNA with me. It was uncanny that she had the same full name as the Dawn I'd driven down to Naples to find and even stranger that they both had friends on their social media sites with the last name of Kavalier.

I still hadn't heard from Macy or Parker, so I sent them another message. Angel, however, was hot on the trail, boldly running ahead of me. Unbeknownst to me, she jumped the gun. She found a young girl named Liz on social media who was friends with both Parker and Macy. They were all related. Angel saw Liz was online at that moment and sent her a message.

"Hello, I am Mary—a volunteer researcher helping my friend Valerie with her genealogy search. She is a first cousin to Macy Kavalier. She has messaged her through Facebook. I would appreciate you contacting Macy to read the message and contact me. I really need your help. Valerie has looked for so long for her family. Thanks for any help." Liz immediately responded to her, asking for my contact information.

Angel told me to get on Messenger and wait to hear from Macy. I did, and then a text from Angel popped up on my cell. "You have a sister!" She sent me a photograph of three women and a man. She didn't know who the man was, but the women were Marilyn and Macy, and she thought the third woman was my sister. Another flash from Angel came in. "You may need to go on a trip soon."

My nails were bitten down to the quick. Angel ran more of her magic searches and found that Marilyn had been married twice and that her second husband, who I'll call Serge, had passed away in Florida. Angel sent me his obituary, saying, "I am 98 percent sure that Marilyn is your mother."

I now had the family names mentioned in the obituary. By running a check on the property tax records for the county listed, I found a house listed in her name, along with another man mentioned in the obit. He had the same surname as Serge. Was he an uncle, cousin, or Holy Toledo, did I have a brother? I discovered he was two years younger than me by running searches on his name. Since he owned the house with her, he had to be my brother. The curtain came down as I tried to fathom that my mother had a daughter two years before me and a son two years after me.

Why was I sandwiched out? What happened that she didn't keep me? I yelled at the top of my lungs, "It's not fair!" The roller coaster was screaming downhill. Both my sister and brother had gone to the same schools as me! Oh God, what if my brother had been a high school infatuation, and we had dated? How crazy is it that I went to school with him and never knew it? I'd heard about genetic attraction, but to be in the middle of that situation hit too close to home.

Marilyn's residence was on the east coast of Florida, not California. I'd searched the west coast for decades, but she had been under my nose all along. She had stayed in Miami after relinquishing me and married Serge soon after that. I assumed she was still alive because the house was still in her name. She'd be in her late nineties, so there was no time to hesitate. I needed to go now.

With her address in hand, I was ready to take off. I called Angel and asked if she wanted to go with me. She said, "I am doing all I can to keep you from going to Florida and knocking on her door." Angel had some things to say about my state of mind and shared her personal experience.

"Valerie, there's an emotional toll that clarity brings. Only now, as I look back over my life, do I realize how much losing my first child changed me. Like a pebble tossed in a pond, the events of that autumn rippled through my life, unconsciously shaping all I thought and did. I constantly question why it took me so long to understand what happened, but I guess it is human nature to shy away from pain."

The crackling of the fire subsided. Staring at the shimmering blood-orange embers, I thought about what she said and tried to imagine what my mother was going through. I didn't know her history or the pain she might have gone through. Was she forced to give me up? Had she told anyone about me? I knew nothing about her state of mind, then or now. She wasn't the young woman that relinquished me over six decades ago. I had to handle this with kid gloves and be sensitive.

Scooting another log onto the fire, I wanted to burn away all the decades of lies and secrets. I tried to be compassionate, but I really wanted to turn on the big spotlights. She might be terrified of being exposed if she carried me as a dark secret all her life.

Night had fallen, and I was famished after not eating anything all day. I gobbled up a cheese sandwich and munched an entire bag of chocolate-covered espresso beans. I was ready for a marathon and brought in more wood for the fire. The night was still young enough to hear from Macy.

23

BEYOND
ALL ODDS

The roaring fire crackled as it devoured the log. Time was running out as I prayed my mother was still alive. I texted Angel that I'd taken her words to heart. Calming down somewhat, I was thinking more rationally, even after devouring all the espresso beans. Despite my years of searching, the ability to wait had never been a strong attribute of mine. While my life was on hold, I delved back into trying to find out more about A.K. She might be my aunt by marrying Uncle Henson or my aunt's daughter.

Messenger chimed on my computer at 9:30 pm, and it was Macy. She'd read my texts and asked how we were related. I gave her my who, what, where, when, and whys and told her that my uncle was Henson Kavalier. She said that was her father. I texted back, "Yes, I know." Immediately she asked for clarification that I was saying her Aunt Marilyn was my mother. I knew my answer would either open the door or seal it. I took a deep breath and typed, "Yes," and at least four deep breaths more to click send. Then I panicked. Was it too late to delete it? Should I try a different approach?

Macy replied that she certainly didn't know about this and didn't think anyone else knew. She wanted to know how I was certain her aunt was my birth mother. By her use of the word "birth mother," I guessed she'd looked through my social media posts. It's not a term that people outside of the adoption triad typically use. That meant Macy must have seen all the pictures I'd posted of myself from age three up to the present. That post read, "In case my biological family finds their way here, I hope you recognize me in these photos."

I told Macy about my three DNA tests. It looked like her father was my uncle, so she must be my first cousin. I told her I didn't believe in the absolute, but I was convinced that her aunt Marilyn was my mother.

Macy said she'd relay my information to her aunt and see how she wanted to handle it. I could barely respond. For the first time in my decades of searching, I knew for sure that my mother was alive! Chills shot up my spine through the top of my head. Macy said she'd contact her aunt in the morning to see what information she'd like to give me. I told her how grateful I was and to call me anytime, night or day. "Is your aunt in Florida too?" I asked.

Yes, my mother was in Florida. I wanted to leave right then and drive straight south through the snow. Curtailing my eagerness, I calmly said, "Thank you so much. Please let her know I'd love to talk to her directly." Macy messaged that she was very protective and only wanted to do what Marilyn was comfortable with. I told Macy she knew best but to please give her aunt my phone number and let her know I'd be grateful if she called me. "Please tell her I've had a good life and that my adopted parents passed many years ago." Macy assured me she'd call after reviewing things with her aunt.

A whirlwind of emotions had me pacing. Angel counseled me to go easy and not come on too strong. At the end of our conversation, she said. "I'm surprised you're not already camping on her lawn!" I knew that if my mother rejected me that I'd still drive down and somehow meet her anonymously. Even if it meant fabricating an elaborate lie, I had to see her face-to-face. How about posing as a delivery person bringing flowers to the wrong address? Better yet, I could pretend my car had broken down in front of her house and ask to use her phone. I'd say my cell battery was dead, and I needed to call AAA. Log after log turned to ashes as I ran different scenarios for a Plan B.

I lit more candles calling for help from the Almighty, Archangel Michael, Mother Mary, my Spirit Guides, and my beloved Gurudev. Asking for help with something so personal was selfish, but I did it anyway. The desire to know my mother was overpowering. I wasn't asking for the greatest good for all concerned. I was pleading for the grace to meet my mother. So be it! Visualizing a wonderful long-awaited reunion, I hopped in bed.

The coffee maker buzzed as the aroma lured me up to stoke the fire. Macy might be talking to my mother right now. If only I could be Siri listening in on their conversation. I got my inner community to focus on positive visualizations. "My mother is inviting me to come and see her right away. I see myself walking up to her with a bouquet of red roses, and she embraces me. She's telling me how wonderful it is that I found her. She wants me to be in her life." That was much better than focusing on Plan B. Affirmations continued as I downed the entire pot of coffee. I was high on expecting the best outcome.

One of my heroes is Albert Einstein. Whenever I opened the fridge to get cream for my coffee, his quote on a magnet inspired me: "**Everything is energy and that's all there is to it. Match the frequency of the reality you want and you cannot help but get that reality. It can be no other way. This is not philosophy, this is physics.**" I had to believe this.

I made more coffee, this time espresso. Supporters and friends called in, and I told everyone right off that I'd have to get off if a call came in. The usual robocalls came, and I had to answer because it could be a call from anyone in my family. Maybe she'd told her children, and they had my number now. The sounds of my phone and computer ricocheted back and forth, announcing calls and messages. I took a deep breath each time before looking to see who it was.

Denial

Finally, Macy sent a message. Without ado, she said she spoke to her aunt. Squeezing my knees together, trying to hold back the pot of espresso I'd drunk, I texted, "Thank you, oh thank you, thank you so much, I'm so grateful." She continued matter-of-factly, saying her aunt did not confirm anything.

My heart sank like a battleship helplessly capsized. "Did you tell her I'd remain a secret, and only the three of us would know?" My keyboard was drowning in tears as I strained to type something sensible. "Sorry, I've worried about how this might affect her. I wanted to connect with her one-to-one to be totally confidential." Macy said she was happy to be the intermediary and would have told her in person if she lived nearby. Her aunt had not revealed how she felt about all this.

There was so much I wanted to know. I didn't dare ask if the man listed on her property record might be my brother. It might scare Macy off if I revealed how much I already knew. I said, "I was ecstatic to see photos of your family on Facebook. Marilyn looks so young and vibrant. In one photo, she had a band-aid on her arm and I'm wondering how she's doing." Macy said she was in quite good health for her age but had back pain.

She asked who my biological father was, and I said that was still a mystery to solve. Macy wanted to know how I connected to her via DNA since she'd never had a test. I explained that her grandson Parker posted a family tree linking my highest DNA match to himself. Macy was baffled about who A.K. might be.

I texted her that I also had information from the state of Florida, where I petitioned for my non-identifying information on two occasions. From that, I learned she had blond hair and blue eyes, like me. It said she was born in the largest far-western coastal state, so I knew it was California. It stated her birthday was about a week after mine. I received a few more clues the second time I petitioned the State. It said that my birth mother's aunt had adopted a child and had considered adopting me as well but thought it might create problems in the family. I hoped Macy might have heard of a great aunt who adopted a child. If she did, she didn't let on. I had figured out who many relatives were but kept mum about contacting anyone.

Macy reiterated this had to be between us for now. I had to be ok with that. My big thumbs texted as fast as possible, "It must be challenging for her to know I've been trying to find her." Send." I sure wish I'd been a fly on the wall when you told her." Send. "Can I have flowers delivered from a secret admirer or something?" Send. "I live in Asheville and would love you both to visit." Clicking send again, I realized I'd not given her enough time to respond to my messages. All that caffeine might not have been a good idea.

Macy said we had to go slow. I apologized for going on and on. I told her it was hard to sit back, not knowing what was happening in her aunt's mind. She said Marilyn had to make the first move, and I needed to be patient and pray. She was going to see her next week. The thought of waiting a week to get any news was excruciating. I told her to call me anytime and gave her my email address.

There was no way to wait for a week. She was my mother, and I was going to see her. Roaming around the house like a lost puppy, I picked up things she might like and made a pile to take with me. I wrote her a letter, then another, and threw them both into the fire. I got out my guitar and composed a song for her. Angel didn't know yet. How could I say anything until I figured out how I felt?

My mother did not admit that I was her baby. Deep wounds of abandonment tore wide open, and the only medicine to ease the pain was to see her. My inner community came to the rescue reminding me how fortunate I was to have finally found her. Against all odds, she was alive, and I'd meet her one way or another. I climbed back into bed and hid under the covers, curling into a fetal position. The waiting was unbearable.

"Not to have knowledge of what
happened before you were born is to be
condemned to live forever as a child."
- Marcus Tullius Cicero (c. 106-43 BC)

24

EXPECTING

The ball was in my mother's court. I called Angel and caught her up to date. I wanted to send flowers, but Macy and Angel thought it wasn't a good idea. Angel said it might look like I was trying to buy my way in. Well, at this point I'd buy my way into the truth if I had to.

Angel confessed she'd sent a message to Macy offering to speak with my mother because she'd probably never spoken to another birth mother. She thought it might help to share a bit of her own story. Angel hadn't told her children to begin with and empathized with my mother on several levels. "You know," she said, "she'll have to tell them about you. If they find out after she's gone, they'll feel betrayed. She needs to release her secret for her own benefit if nothing else. But it isn't easy. It was traumatic for my children to discover I'd held the secret all their lives. There was no way I could talk with my daughter until I told my other children."

Angel always seemed to know what to say to ease my tension. I imagined being found by your secret baby was scary enough. If my mother knew how much I now knew and how I'd come to know it, she might feel threatened and stalked. Angel said, "I need you to remain calm and not jump into anything. Let's hope your mother calls Macy tomorrow and doesn't wait."

Fingers crossed, I decided an epsom salt bath was in order. At least I'd be calm if Macy called again or if my mother had prepared to talk to me directly. Just in case, I set my phone and computer within reach of my tub. I thought about how my mother felt in the hospital or wherever she was when she was expecting me. The ecstatic expectancy I had waiting to hear her voice had to be just as laborious. Did she talk to me in her womb? Had she wished I was a boy so I could take care of myself? Would I recognize her voice from some faint womb memory? I wanted to ask her so many things. I felt like a little girl. You know, the one who follows her mother around saying, "Mommy, Mommy," until she gets her attention.

I've been accused of acting childish many times in my life. I always thought that growing up was a trap. Gurudev said, "A child is like a saint without knowledge. A saint is like a child with knowledge." Maybe I was somewhere in between. Perhaps my personality developed from a pathological imprint from a previous life or at birth, keeping me in a habitual childlike state. Intense childhood experiences cause deep impressions and affect our personalities, perspectives, and reactions. Like any unconscious habitual pattern, it can help us evolve or bring us down. Or, in my case, up and down like a yo-yo.

Regardless of what psychics and the saint at the Brighu readings told me, I had no experiential past-life knowledge. What past karmas might have created abandonment by my mother? Maybe I abandoned a baby and needed to know what that was like. Or did I need to be independent, without family ties, in order to carry out my life's work? I didn't know, but I imagined my issues arose from my birth trauma. And what about my mother? What were her karmas? Since I hadn't figured out mine, how could I understand hers?

Curiosity fuels my creativity, but sometimes it drives me bananas. My bath relaxed my body, but not my monkey mind. I couldn't get my thoughts, feelings, and emotions on the same page. I knew they all had to be in unison to make any affirmation effective. As much as I tried, I still hadn't dropped all the judgments and negative feelings that bubbled up. Then there were my judgments about myself for having judgments. I needed more compassion for myself.

In the meantime, I had to embrace the chaos and keep busy. I cleared everything out of Silver Wing, my trusty 2000 Honda CRV. Then she got a vacuum job and a bath. She hadn't looked this classy in years. My adoptive mom always said that sweeping or creating something of beauty would keep pandemonium at bay. At that moment, her wise words spurred me into creating an altar on my dashboard and preparing a plush seat for my mother. There was no doubt she'd be sitting next to me soon.

What might I wear to meet her? My biological family dressed upscale in the pictures I'd seen. I pulled all my summery clothes from the back of my closet and put on one outfit after another, looking in the mirror and rejecting them all. Why was I being so vain? They'd have to take me as I was. I wondered if my mother had even seen my little naked body after having me. Had she ever even touched me?

I wrote a letter to my mother and Macy, summarizing my search to strengthen my case. Just reading all I'd done was exhausting. Touching base with my supporters, I brought them up to speed. Having them rooting for me boosted my courage. It was too late for Macy to respond or for anyone else to call. Retreating to the comfort of my fort, I piled up pillows on each side of me, leaving room for my headlight, journal, water bottle., and computer on my lap. I kept searching for more information until the words on my screen looked like a hallucination of building blocks. How many nights would I be doing this?

I awoke early with pain in my neck and a numb arm. My fort was strewn over the side of my bed, billowing onto the floor, including my computer. Fortunately, my down comforter had softened the scuffle, and my digital brain wasn't damaged. I slathered arnica, my go-to for pain, all over my aching body and made some espresso.

A message from Macy came in. She was amazed at all I had done but said we had to wait and let her aunt Marilyn come around on her own terms without any pressure. She said she knew it was hard to wait now that I'd found her. Her words were a pivotal point in my psyche. Knowing she believed me helped still my mind.

A message from Angel popped up. "Any word yet? I'm so nervous for you." Calling her, I filled her in on the exciting details. She was almost as impatient as I was. Setting my laptop operations up in my sunroom, I drafted an email to Macy.

"Macy, thank you so much for your support. You've been so kind and welcoming. The emotions I'm having are something I wasn't prepared for. I'm sure my mother is also processing a lot. Knowing who I am and where I came from is such a blessing. Just looking into her face in a picture gives me a sense of who I am. I have her phone number now, but I won't make any contact. I'm praying she'll open her heart to me."

That seemed right and I clicked send. My mother didn't have email, which was probably good, or I might have blown it. I only had to monitor my phone, which I carried around in my kangaroo pocket sweatshirt as if my life depended on it. That probably wasn't great health-wise because of the EMFs, but I didn't want to risk misplacing it.

What can I call my mother?

I didn't even know what to call her. "Birth mother" didn't seem right. Calling her "Marilyn" didn't work for me either. How about "natural mother"? But that means my mother, who raised me, was unnatural. It seemed disrespectful and mean to refer to her as unnatural. What about "first mother"? But wouldn't that mean my adoptive mother was a stepmother? If I called her "Mother," wouldn't that be disrespectful to my adoptive mother?

I toyed around with "Mommy," imagining I'd have called her that if she'd cradled me. But that felt way too emotionally charged. I thought about "Mum," but that had the connotation of keeping a secret. I'd been a secret my entire life, and I didn't want to reinforce that. And how would I speak of her with my new siblings? It was too alienating to have to say "your mother." She was mine too! I'm sure many adoptees face this dilemma in reunion.

I needed to come up with something totally different. I scribbled down ideas like Mamarilyn, Mother Nature, and Mama Mia. Everything sounded weird or wasn't adaptable to every situation. I needed to call her something. It sounded too Italian for our DNA, but for now, I settled on "Mama Mia" and wrote a song for her. I planned to sing it to her if she let me into her life. Correction: when she lets me into her life.

Singing my "Mama Mia" song over and over, I shuffled through the enormous piles of search files and made a folder to take with me. By the time I finished, Mama Mia sounded too much like a joke. Back to square one. Wondering what the word "mother" actually meant, I googled for a definition, and the first ones I found were: "1. The woman who gave birth to you; 2. The person who brings you up 3. A stringy slime that forms on the surface of fermenting liquids."

Well, she didn't bring me up, and I hoped she wasn't slimy. In India, the Sanskrit word used for mother is *Mataa*. Gurudev said it was from the vibrational sound that birthed existence. Remembering that, I thought calling her Mother or Mataa was fair enough. Since my adopted mother passed, I didn't think she'd mind. I narrowed it down to Mother Marilyn or Mother Maata. The initials of either one were M.M., and that became my nickname for her. It rolled off my tongue like a sweet M&M.

Angel texted me a different picture of someone she thought was my sister, along with a name. OMG, how many sisters did I have? I called Angel immediately while googling the name. She didn't answer, but another message came in. It was a picture of a handsome guy standing by a fancy car, and her text said, "I think this is your brother." I sat breathless, trying to grasp that I had a brother and maybe more than one sister. I finally got through to Angel and jabbered on and on about the discovery. She finally got me centered and gave me advice on how to proceed.

An alert popped up on my screen. Macy had good news. Her aunt Marilyn called, and they talked over everything. She had my number and would call me in the next few days after gathering her thoughts. Macy was excited for all of us and signed off with, "take care cuz."

Hallelujah! She called me cuz, so I knew I was in.

The Excruciating Wait

I wanted to be ready for MM's call at any time, so I slid my phone, notepad, pen, snacks, and flashlight into my kangaroo pocket, stuffing it to the max. Passing a mirror, I looked as if I were pregnant. I wondered how my mother felt carrying me in her belly.

I got my workout bag and emptied it, except for two dumbbell weights. My birth certificate didn't say how much I weighed at birth, but I thought ten pounds was ample. Hanging it around my neck wasn't too bad. I crossed my hands over my belly bag and walked around the room. I'd seen many pregnant women hold their hands in the same position. Were they cradling babies in their wombs, or was it to help them walk? The extra weight on my belly naturally made me want to hold the weight up as I walked. But even then, I needed to take small steps to walk with ease. To do that for months seemed daunting.

Macy got back to me that evening, recommending I take slow baby steps for now. Marilyn was a private person, and Macy was concerned I'd overwhelm her. I agreed to take baby steps ... after all, my mother had never seen me walk. She had to take baby steps before having me, and I'd do it now. I lived with my kangaroo pocket stuffed, minus the dumbbells, day and night, waiting for a call.

Day 1. It was already nightfall, but I thought it might still happen at any minute. Macy said her aunt would call me within the next few days. That might be now, right? I switched my phone ringer to a loud blues riff and re-checked that my computer was ready to record. I didn't want to miss a single word of this vital call.

Pacing the house, I cleaned things as they crossed my path to keep my emotional gyrations at bay. If she visited me, my house had to be sparkling clean. Colonies of dust bunnies awaited in nooks and crannies I'd never seen before. From ceiling to floor, I did a winter-spring cleaning that any mother would be proud of.

What would I say when she called? I experimented with, "Hi, I'm so thrilled you called," or, "I've been waiting a lifetime for this moment." That felt too vulnerable. What if she called to tell me to stay away? Perhaps being aloof was better: "Who's calling, please?" I wasn't able to settle on anything. I scribbled more notes on what I wanted to know and pondered how to ask questions. Gorging on ice cream and snacks, I was buzzed wide awake. At about three in the morning, I ran a long charger cord to reach my bedside table and plugged in my phone and computer.

Day 2

I don't remember sleeping, but I awoke to a lively dawn chorus of birds. Butterflies fluttered in my stomach with thoughts of the joy of hearing her voice for the first time. Heading to brew up my caffeine fix, the blues riff announced a call. It was from Florida. Dashing to my computer, I dug in my pocket for my notes. Damn it, they must have fallen out during the night. There was no time to locate them now. Oh God, what would I say?

I answered in the calmest voice I could muster and simply said, "Good morning." Shit, it was another robocall about a student loan. I never had a student loan. Do they imagine every person that went to college has one?

The day found me canceling one calendar agenda after another. I had to be in the sanctuary of my home to get this call. I experimented with how far I could go with my phone and still be able to get back to my computer within three rings. A girlfriend helped and called me over and over until I knew my limits.

Grabbing a bag of peanuts, I walked out on the deck to toss the hulls overboard. It was the warmest weather in days, so I wandered out to the garden to see what was left to graze on. Standing there with an armful of mustard greens, the blues riff went off. Ohhh no! I raced back to the house at double speed but missed the call. Fortunately, it had been a friend calling to check on me. I didn't leave the house for the rest of the day. Angel called and was privy to my mind's burning questions. Would I recognize my birth mother's voice from some primal embryonic listening ability in her womb? Would she have kept me had I been a boy? What if she denied I was hers? Questions bombarded me like falling black walnuts.

Back on the deck, I cracked open the last few peanuts. The western sky turned blood red as the chill of the evening enveloped me. I wondered if my mother liked peanuts too. Were my tastes inherited? Another robo call came in, and a restless night ensued, with the periodic exhilaration of racing to the computer for another disappointment.

Day 3. The Appalachian mist billowed through the oak tree branches hanging over my deck. Rubbing the early morning dew on my face, a cloud of fear seeped in. Maybe she wouldn't call. She was probably as nervous as I was … and scared. If some guy had gotten her pregnant and left, or she was raped, it'd be a nightmare. I needed to give both of us reassurance and compassion.

Remembering the adoptee retreat in the Virgin Islands brought me back to what I'd learned about first contact and reunions. We were told to prepare for the worst possible scenario. To me, it seemed counterproductive to imagine negative scenarios. Maybe I was in denial, but I chose to visualize a heartwarming reunion.

I remember nervously waiting my turn to walk over hot coals in Chile once, but the last two days were harder than that. What does "a few days" mean? I thought it meant two. I looked up the word "few" and didn't find a helpful answer. I was chain-drinking coffee, imagining my mother loved it too. I ate everything I could swallow easily, ready to answer the phone. My perspective see-sawed from what I wanted to ask her to wondering how she felt. Realizing that Macy now knew her big secret might be traumatic. Maybe she was infuriated that I tracked her down. Catching my negative thoughts before they could run any further, I turned on classical piano music to trick my monkey mind into thinking I was calm.

Day Four

The band I sang with, "The Tameless," was rehearsing for a gig. I sent a message saying I wouldn't be there as I was waiting for the call. They finally convinced me that when she did call, I could let it ring and call back when I got home.

I dressed and swung back and forth between "Yes, I'm going" to "No way." At the last possible minute, I walked out the back door and jumped in the car. Backing up, my phone rang. Leaving the car running, I bolted to the door, frantically punched in the lock code, and skidded through the community laundry room into the kitchen. Reaching the island counter, I knew I had to answer without making it to my computer. The caller was from Florida!

I braced myself, took a deep breath, and answered calmly. "Hello?" Silence was on the other end. "Hello," I said again, louder, and still got no response. Thinking it might be another robocall, I yelled, "Hello, is anyone there?" I was about to hang up when I realized the sound on my phone was off. Damn, I'd been so prepared, and now this! I clicked to unmute the sound and heard a woman yelling at me.

Loud and clear, there was no mistake. My mind dropped into emptiness with no words to respond. A silence that seemed like an eternity enveloped me, and then she said it again.

"This is your mommy!"

25

FIRST CONTACT

Those first four words are embedded in my heart. I was in my sixth decade and felt like a two-year-old. What finally came out of my mouth after hearing, "This is your mommy," was an apology. I said something like, "Oh, I'm so sorry, the sound was off on my phone. I really wanted to contact you directly. This must have been an enormous shock to hear I was looking for you."

Damn ... I wasn't recording yet. Staying focused on the call, I heard her say yes, she'd been in shock, but Macy encouraged her to call me and promised I wouldn't tell her family. Assuring her I wouldn't divulge her secret I made it to my computer and clicked record. Hearing her voice was like hearing myself talk. I told her I'd waited a lifetime to talk to her and didn't want to miss a single word. "I'm going to record us so we can hear it all over again, ok?" She laughed and said, "You can do whatever you want Valerie. Macy said you're a gracious lady."

Being called a lady shook me out of my childlike state. She apologized for taking so long to reach out. I told her I wanted to know all about her life and asked how she ended up in Florida. She wanted to hear about me, and I told her I grew up in Miami. "Is that where I was born?" I asked.

Her stark words were, "I don't remember anything. I don't remember going to a hospital and I don't remember all the pain you gave me. I just remember handing you over to some nice couple. Were your parents good to you?"

My chest collapsed into a gaping hole. Pushing my hand flat against my breast I tried to hold myself together. Exposed, vulnerable, and frightened, I had to stop whatever was tunneling into me. Trying to carry on the conversation, I pulled my knees to my chest and said, "Yes, my adopted parents were good people, but they passed when I was young, and they never talked about my adoption."

How could she not remember having me? I've never had a baby, but it's unbelievable that a woman wouldn't remember birthing her own flesh and blood. And to say she didn't remember all the pain I gave her! That statement pierced through my core. She blamed her pain on me? The thought of an infant being responsible for her pain was more than I could take in. I slid the phone a few inches away, needing to distance myself. Crossing my arms, holding on to my shoulders, I rocked back and forth in my office chair. The sensations were totally foreign to me. It was all I could do to say, "I've had a great life." She addressed me as "honey" and said how wonderful that was. "What do you do?" she asked.

Hugging myself with all my might, I gave her a brief rundown and said I was now a gardener of life. I told her I was pretty stubborn, not taking money from my parents for my education because I wanted to put myself through college on my own. "Oh, my goodness, Valerie, how did you do that?"

I told her about the place called 1520 AD on Miami Beach and rattled on about my adventures as a costumed serving wench. "I drew cleavage on my chest because I didn't have large breasts." She giggled like a little girl, and it amazed me how youthful she sounded. I sang her part of a wenching song I'd performed: "All I want is a room somewhere, far away from the cold night air." Here I was, entertaining again like I did for my adoptive parents and Gurudev. It was uncanny that her laugh was so much like mine.

I told her I hadn't left home for three days, waiting to hear from her. "I don't even know what to call you. Since I'm a secret, what do you think?" That wasn't supposed to be a funny question, but she chuckled and said, "You're my daughter Valerie, and you can call me mommy or mother or whatever you want to." I said, "Awwww Mommy thank you. How about Mommy Marilyn or better yet, a sweet secret nickname to stand for that, like M&M?" Cackling even louder, she loved it.

She said she was sorry we had to be a secret, and she'd been so worried about me finding her. Letting her grandchildren know that she gave a baby away was out of the question. She said it took a lot of nerve for her to call me. She was only going to send me pictures but said to herself, you're a chicken. You have got to just pick up the phone and call. She kept putting it off and finally got the guts to do it today. I commended her braveness and said, "Now I know where I got my courage from." But my mind nailed her as a scared chicken running from the truth.

I stuffed my judgments and despair of her not remembering my birth deep into some hidden vault. I wanted the truth, and I was getting it.

"So, how was your life, Valerie? You seem to have done okay." she said. I summoned my mature self and told her my life had been wonderful. I filled her in about leaving the fast life of the film industry and moving to Asheville. She asked more questions before I could ask her one.

She wanted to know about me. I'd heard so many stories of adoptees being re-rejected. She'd opened up to me, and that was huge. Softly, seeming more authentic, she said how happy she was to get to know me. "Valerie, you have been in my mind for many years."

Hearing that stopped my nervous rocking. My shoulders sank down below my ears as my tension eased. When there was space in the conversation, I told her about my fainting spells and asked if she had ever fainted. "Mine always came on when visiting someone in the hospital. Do you think that's related to my birth?" She said she'd never fainted and repeated that she remembered nothing about my birth except handing me over. I said, "It must have been hard for you to give me up." She actually laughed and said, "Ohhhhh no." And then my world totally stopped as she told me something I was entirely unprepared for.

"I want to tell you that your father was trying to find you for a long time."

Who is my father?

The ecstatic grief of hearing that my birth father looked for me shattered my illusions. All these years, I'd characterized him as a villain. Reduced to a puddle of shame, I wanted to find him and tell him how sorry I was. I loved him without knowing who he was. I begged her to tell me about him. "He was something else. He really was a wonderful guy, but I think he loved me too much."

There had to be more to this. I told her about finding my Adoption Decree that referred to me as Infant Hanson and that I'd searched for decades thinking that was her last name.

"Is Hanson his name?" I asked, "Is my father a Hanson?" She said, "Oh yes, he was very handsome. He was so good looking."

I might have thought that was funny if I hadn't been so emotional. I tried to get more from her, but she wanted to hear about my life. I gave her a brief recap of my business endeavors in Asheville. She was intrigued by my entrepreneurship with Carolina Costumes and the balloon business. She said it was unbelievable that she had such a smart kid.

I told her about designing my house on the Ivy River and at Earthaven, and she said my father was a builder. I was betting my skills came from him. "Was your handsome builder named Hanson?" I asked. I didn't want to push her, but my inner community badgered me for an answer. She hemmed and hawed and finally said, "I forget what it was. I'll tell you later."

It may not be hard to forget an old boyfriend's name, but to forget who you had a baby with seemed far-fetched. What was she hiding? I told her about registering with numerous groups that would match me with her if she ever searched for me. She said emphatically that she never looked for me.

I went on and told her about petitioning the state of Florida for non-identifying information. "The information said you were from the largest western coastal state, so I knew it was California. It also said your birthday was about a week after mine. I thought I'd find you with that info, but there were no Hanson matches. The report also mentioned that you'd considered giving me to your aunt because she'd adopted a child. I'm wondering if that's true and who she is." She said her aunt Elmira had adopted two children. But she wasn't sure about the details because it was so long ago. I told her not to worry that my memory abandons me at times too.

"My hope," I said, "is that we can have a relationship. Finding you has been a lifelong calling." She said she was only worried about her family knowing who I was. I assured her I wouldn't expose myself and asked to come and see her. An uneasy silence followed.

She began rambling on about her family again, telling me how talented her granddaughter was and how good a fisherman her grandson was. I stiffened up as she went on and on about "her" family. I'm her own flesh and blood. Didn't she have any empathy for what I'd been through? But I couldn't let myself slide into a "poor pitiful me" during this crucial first conversation.

Playing my part, I said, "I will never cause any trouble in the family, that's for sure. It was great connecting with Macy. She's a kindred soul, and it wouldn't be a lie to say Macy and I are friends who went to the same high school. That can be our coverup story. I was floored to find out we went to high school together."

She continued talking about all her family and how wonderful her grandchildren were. I'd be kidding myself if I said I didn't feel like a pouting alien outcast. Tears slid down my face tumbling onto a picture of her on my desk. Wiping it off with my sleeve made things worse. M&M heard me and said, "Don't do that. Please don't cry. Oh, I'm so sorry honey." I told her I'm not typically emotional but not to worry as I was crying tears of joy. I lied.

She asked where I'd lived in Miami, and I told her I grew up a block from Miami High, and then later, my adopted mother got breast cancer, and we moved to Hialeah. She didn't respond to any of that. Instead, she came out with, "Oh, my goodness, I must tell you something. I was the May Queen in high school."

I retorted by telling her I was Miss Teenage Miami. Her granddaughter, she said, saw pictures of her as the May Queen with the King and asked her why she didn't marry him. He was so cute, she said, and then got on her computer trying to find him.

After hearing a few more family stories, I jumped in and asked, "How do you feel about me coming down to see you? I already found a place close by to stay. Once I'm there we can decide how to spend some time together. I won't be any bother. I've dreamed of seeing you face to face my entire life."

My stiffness collapsed when she said, "Oh, wouldn't that be nice. I would love it. I've been thinking about you a lot and Macy says you're terrific."

Through tears of joy this time, I sobbed, "You have no idea how long I've thought about you, and yes I want to see you as soon as possible." Then she demanded I stop whimpering.

Staying on track, I said, "How about if I come Monday?" She hesitated and said she had some things planned already. "Or how about Tuesday?" I asked. She laughed and said she had to check her calendar. I let her know I'd canceled everything on my agenda to be free to travel. She began rattling off things on her calendar and then suggested November. I asked her about Wednesday, the first day of November. That was less than a week away. She said she had three things on her schedule that first week but would be free the following week.

"I'll have my own place down there," I said. "There are lots of other things I can do when you're busy. I can drive down Halloween day and see you whenever you want in November."

"Let me see," she said, "hold on a minute." I could almost hear her looking through her calendar. "Monday, oh, that's when my friend visits, and oh dear, another friend comes over. Wednesday. Oh, and my first cousin's birthday is Friday, and we're having a party at my house." Impatiently I ask, "How about if I drive on Wednesday anyway and check in with you when I get there? I'll be in the area, and we can work something out without any stress."

To my surprise, she said maybe she would cancel some appointments. I wanted to jump in the car right then. She told me her cousin was a singer and played in a band and how much I'd like him. Then with the grace of the Almighty, she said, "Okay, let's try for Wednesday, the first of November."

I bounced up, shaking off all my doubts. "I'm thrilled to be able to see you, and I'll call when I'm on the way." She said if I wanted to just come to her house, nobody would know the difference. I asked what would happen if someone did come over. In her best queen-like demeanor, she said, "I'm not going to let that happen."

I told her I had her address posted up on my wall, along with many photos. "I have so much information about you plastered on my walls, my friends think I'm crazy." She burst out laughing and said, "Oh, you sure are!" She gave me the codes to get through the main security gate to get to her house, and I told her if I couldn't get in, I'd probably climb the gate. We laughed the same way again, in perfect sync.

"What can I bring you? What's your favorite drink? In every picture I've seen, you have a cocktail in your hand. I thought to bring a nice bottle of wine or champagne to celebrate our reunion."

Laughing hysterically this time, she squealed, "Oh my God, you think I'm an alcoholic. You know, I'm not, but whenever we go out, we have a drink. You just come. You don't have to bring anything except your pictures. I can't wait to see you. I really am looking forward to this."

I told her how blissed and blessed I was to hear her voice and for us to have this chance to get to know each other.

She said, "You know, Valerie, I've been blessed in my life, and you finding me is another good thing that's happened. You're going to stay with me. There's no reason why you can't. It's not going to be a problem. I'll just introduce you as a friend." I reminded her that we could say I'm Macy's friend and keep it a secret between the three of us, and she agreed. But in the back of my mind, I was freaking out about how deep in layers of lies this secret might take us.

"You're less than ten hours' drive from me," I said. "That's not much, considering I traveled to Naples last year on a wild goose chase, thinking I'd find you there. Do you know someone with the initials A.K.? You're related, but I'm not sure how." She had no idea who that was.

"I'll tell you about my searching escapades when I get there if you like." She wanted to hear all about it and demanded I stay for at least a week. I was her lucky charm; she'd had a lucky streak since Macy told her about me. "We're going to have a fun time," she said. "I've thought about you for a long time."

"I've thought about you throughout my life. I imagined it was hard for you and that your parents made you give me up."

"No," she whispered. "They didn't even know."

I told her there was so much I'd imagined throughout the years that were off kilter." I'll see you soon M&M. I look forward to our first hug and I'll call you tomorrow."

Her reply was the best part of my entire search. "Me too. See you soon Valerie ... I love you."

26

THE SECRET PLAN

I couldn't have asked for more than to hear her say, "I love you." That was nothing my imagination had rehearsed. I was already mostly packed, so I spent the weekend catching up with friends, writing, and trying to chill out. I found out from Macy that my mother did yoga every day. She still drove her car and was amazingly active. At 94, she lived alone and was so independent. We seemed so much alike, and I was ecstatic to have such great genes.

By Monday, I was too beside myself to stay home. I took off as a stunning sunset settled down on the mountain ridges. I was driving off into this glorious landscape to see my mother for the first time in my life.

Since I'd left two days early, I took some back roads to pace myself. As I crossed into Georgia, a cute old 1960s motel caught my eye, and I stopped for the night. The woman at the counter was chatty, and I ended up telling her the reason for my trip. Then she confided in me that she had given up her baby girl 24 years ago because of pressure from her family. She'd never told anyone about it before, not even her friends. She went to a secret home for unwed mothers where she had to work for her keep. It sounded awful.

I reached out and embraced her as she opened up and wept. She had thought about her daughter every day, and hearing my story she asked me how to find her. I told her it was easier now because DNA tests were readily available. I wrote down some resources and explained how to go about it. She profusely thanked me for coming to her little motel and sharing so intimately.

She wasn't around when I went in for coffee in the morning, but I left my contact info and a note to call if she needed help. As I left, Angel texted, "Ready to head out?"

I called Angel with an update letting her know I was already on the road. She wanted to talk about my reunion. Angel knew a lot of things I didn't. She'd given her baby girl up for adoption. Her daughter found her. and she was terrified. She had to tell her family before returning the call to her daughter. Angel's story gave me a deeper perspective on what might be going on for my mother. She was probably scared.

I took my time, stopping often to write and process my myriad of strange feelings. As I rolled into Florida, the radio played "Don't Stop Believing." Then "Momma I'm Coming Home" came on. It seemed every song on the radio was playing just for me.

I stopped at a welcome station for coffee, and a brochure for The Monkey Jungle was on the counter. Was the universe playing jokes on me? I stuck it in my purse to show M&M and tell her about my fictitious birth story. Coffee in hand, I sat on a sunny bench and journaled for an hour before heading further south.

Premonition?

After another beautiful sunset, I pulled into a motel and took a long hot bath. Getting a good night's sleep seemed important, but dumbly I turned on the TV. The scenes of horror around the world were anything but relaxing. I woke up from a creepy dream during the night, thinking it might be a premonition. I had reached her house undetected in the dream, and she quickly ushered me in. She was sweetly aloof and gave me some orange juice. I got deathly sick and ended up in a hospital, where I died. She had poisoned me!

Was I blind not to see why our meeting had to be so secretive? I tossed and turned, thinking about the horrendous dream until daylight. I didn't want to tell Angel. She was thrilled about this day, and I didn't want to ruin it with these negative thoughts. I relayed the dream to two close friends and told them I'd probably be in big trouble if they hadn't heard from me in six hours.

A supernova wouldn't stop me from going, but I'd take precautions. My plan was not to eat or drink anything while I was there. I'd tell her my friends were checking in with me and make it seem like I was being watched. I hated that these eerie thoughts had snaked into my euphoric journey. Besides my anxiety about the reunion, fear was now part of the mix. Then it dawned on me that what I had watched on TV before I went to bed must have affected my dreams. The bloodshed and murders could have altered my psyche. Also, it was Halloween, and scaring people was the name of the game.

Halloween has always been an intense time for me. It was the bread and butter of my costume business. All the worry of keeping up with order deadlines, and fretting about how clients would like their getups, was naught in the end. Halloween always turned out successful in every way. So maybe Halloween was my lucky day. I was going to count on that.

Gurudev said that dreams are a way of working things out, so they don't have to occur in the waking state. That must have been what happened. Somehow, I was afraid I'd be abandoned again, that my mother would try to keep me away, so her secret wasn't exposed. I journaled about the dream until I overcame the fear. Then I courageously catapulted myself into the unknown.

Angel texted about my paternal siblings. Like the DNA wizard she was, Angel had already emailed me pictures. The man she thought was my father stood behind two women about my age. She didn't know his name yet, but said the women were my half-sisters Logan and Brenda! Logan was the alias last name I used to get a bank account when moving to NC. I told Angel the Lostar Marbles Logan story and the overlapping synchronicities amped up.

The incredible possibilities ahead danced me back onto the highway. Driving in a daydream of two sisters and a brother, time evaporated. About an hour out from my reunion, Angel texted that she was wrong about my father and sisters. She said she'd work more on it the next day but that I needed to not think about it and totally focus on my reunion. I tried, but how could I not think about it?

First Hug

I picked up a dozen red roses and arrived at the gatehouse. Angel, with impeccable timing, texted, "The day has come that you dreamed about all your life. This is also the beginning of National Adoption Month. I can't wait to hear you are together. The entire universe will shift today. This is my last message, but know I am with you in spirit every step of the way. I don't want you to get distracted, but I think your real siblings' names are Deanna and Nic."

I pulled over to re-read her message. But she was right, my mother expected me any minute, and there was no time to think about anything else. The guardhouse was empty, so I drove right in and followed my GPS around a large lake to her home. Pulling into her driveway, I was prepared for the worst but envisioned the best.

I called to say I'd arrived, and the garage doors opened. There she was, waving at me, dressed all in red with a matching baseball cap half-cocked to the side of her head. She motioned for me to park next to her car. Waving back, I tucked my old trusty silver CRV next to her bright new golden Honda. With roses in hand, I got out and walked up to her. "They match you perfectly!" I said, holding out the bouquet. Laughing, she asked how I knew that red roses were her favorite. "Oh, I have my ways. You know this is quite the special delivery service, and after coming all this way, I deserve a big hug."

I reached out for her, and she opened her arms. The embrace was a time out of time. I'd waited for this moment for so long. I didn't want it to end. I wanted the lifetime's worth of hugs I'd missed. However, all too quickly, she pulled away.

"Did they let you hug me when I was born, or was that our first hug ever?" She laughed and spun on her sneakers back in the house.

"If you forgot the wine, go home.", read the sign above her door. "Hey M&M, I didn't forget the wine, I brought red and white." She said, "Wine will be for later, but let's have coffee now." I jumped in to help make it, and she demanded I sit down, adding, "I'm kinda bossy, huh?"

Laughing back at her, I said, "So am I. I wonder where I got that from."

"Oh boy," she said, "we're in trouble." She gave me a choice of mugs, and I took one with a queen and castle on it. She said, "You may not know it, but I'm the queen." I retorted with, "Yeah, well I'm a queen too."

She turned glaring at me saying, "Oh God, we're going to fight!"

"Actually," I said, "neither of us is married, right? So, we're both princesses." She asked if I wanted to see her crown so I'd know who the real queen was. Without waiting for my reply, she strutted off to find it. She reappeared wearing a pink paper crown her granddaughter had made. I finally conceded and agreed she was the queen and I'd be the princess.

She sat across from me at her round table next to a bay window and waved at people walking by. She was so lucky, she said, to be loved and watched out for. Her son and daughter call every day, and she has the most adorable grandchildren. She pranced into the living room retrieving a drawing of a boat her granddaughter had made, exclaiming how artistic she was.

I nodded and managed a smile while my emotions played ping pong. I felt like an understudy waiting offstage in the dark to step into a role as her daughter. On one hand, I felt loved because she let me into her life. On the other, I felt like a doormat being used for target shooting. I listened as she went on and on about her wonderful grandchildren. As much as I wanted to know about the family, my own little girl was trying to pull out the arrows hitting the core of my being.

She took me on a tour through the house, starting in the living room with wall-to-wall windows overlooking the lake.

Following her to see three bedrooms, she offered me whichever one I wanted to stay in. I chose one with an enormous window looking out on the tranquil water where a white bird stood at its edge. The bed was covered with stuffed animals because that was the room her grandchildren loved to stay in.

Black Jaguar

After unpacking my car, we rested on her enormous wraparound couch. She threw me a leopard-print pillow identical to one I had in my living room at home, along with a matching blankie. I glanced at the mantle over her media center, and a sculpture mesmerized me.

"I'm curious," I said, walking over to it. "Is that a black jaguar?"

"Yes, take it down, she said, I want to tell you about it." I carefully gathered it into my hands, lost in flashbacks of the jaguar dream and my journey on the Amazon River.

"That was a gift from your father," she said, "and I'm sure he would like you to have it now." The world exploded behind my eyelids. His hands must have been where mine were now. Caressing the jaguar's smooth ceramic curves conjured up my medicine's power. I imagined my father watching me accept this legacy. Pressing my lips to the jaguar's head, I inhaled the mystery of his scent. I'd never been this close to my father before.

My dream spell broke when she began laughing again. "What are you doing, Valerie?" I told her I was tuning into the ancestral juju of the gift and shared stories of how the jaguar had been a recurring theme in my life. Inspecting every inch, I turned it over to feel the bottom of his paws. There were four holes that must have been from its mold. "Look," I said, "Maybe he left me a message inside." I gently shook it, hoping to hear something, then slid my pinky into each opening as far as I could, probing for a hidden treasure. Not finding anything, I wondered if she was telling the truth.

She went to get herself a drink, and I did a quick web search with a picture of the sculpture. Sure enough, it was a vintage mid-century piece. She pranced back to the couch, and our blue eyes met in recognition. I trusted myself, and I had to trust her. Caressing my jaguar, I pleaded, "Please, my dear queen, tell me my father's name."

Her response was, "Oh, you must be hungry."

"Yes, I'm hungry. I'm hungry for the truth. Please tell me who he is."

She giggled and said, "Let's go out to dinner."

She went to change her clothes, and I sent a message to my supporters that I was safe and would check in later.

We decided on Italian cuisine since that was both of our favorites. Our mannerisms and lifestyles were so similar. Her spirit of independence in her nineties was remarkable. After a few glasses of wine, I decided just to focus on getting to know her better and dropped my birth father interrogation. I asked her to tell me about my sister and brother.

My sister Deanna, she said, was three years older than me. She lived a few hours away but made it a point to see her every other week. "Why did you name her Deanna?" I asked. She said her first husband's name was Dean, and she gave her Anna as a middle name because that was her best friend's name. The waitress brought our dinner, and I didn't want to spoil it by asking my next question. Was she married to Dean when I was conceived?

"What about your son?" I asked. "Oh, Nic lives minutes from me," she said, "He's a mainstay, but he's too possessive of me. He comes at least once a week and checks on me."

Nic was three years younger than me, and I surmised he was Serge's son. I'd seen Nic's name on the property records as a co-owner of her house.

She said Nic's son Chris lived in the Outer Banks in North Carolina. He was a fisherman, just like his father and her brother. Chris had just left for Costa Rica to spend the winter with his wife and daughter. He was the captain of a fishing boat down there.

I piped up, "I was a sailor and lived on a boat for three years." She skipped over the subject, telling me I'd love her granddaughter Corrie because she was so talented that she could do anything. Confused, I asked if she meant her great-granddaughter. "Well, so what," she pouted, "I call her my granddaughter."

She went on to tell me stories about how clever Corrie was as I stuffed my emotions behind tight lips. She said how lucky she was to have such a wonderful family. "Macy was here yesterday checking up on me and is such a good girl. You know, her mother, Anna, was my best friend and she married my brother. Macy and Deanna were born in the same year and grew up together. Macy's known me her whole life. Her son and grandson work for Disney. We've had so much fun going on their cruises."

I invited her to visit Asheville and bring anyone else she wanted. She said she'd love to but didn't think it'd be possible. She didn't want to travel anymore as she knew her limitations, and Macy had a husband to care for. I asked her, "Isn't it important for women to get away from their men sometimes?"

She laughed, shaking loose her forkful of spaghetti. I jumped up and cleaned her blouse with a wet napkin. We enjoyed our time together, and I cherished every moment.

She asked about my love life, and I told her I didn't have one and that I never really trusted men. "Maybe it had to do with not knowing who my father was," I said. "I imagined he was a jerk, and you had to give me up for adoption because he left you."

"Oh no!" she said. "He proposed to me on the beach, but I thought he loved me too much. You have no idea how much. That's the reason why he tried to find you. You know, he really did love you."

"Did he ever even see me?" I asked. "Was his name Hanson?"

She said she didn't know anyone by that name. Why wouldn't she tell me who he was? Did she need to ask him? Was he younger than her? Was I asking the wrong question?

I thought I was Dutch for many years because of the wooden clogs and trinkets my parents gave me, and then I found a Dutch name on my adoption decree. I asked her, "Do you think my dad Jules, made that Hanson name up?" She said, "He must have. Believe me, honey, I'm telling you everything, but I never knew anyone by that name. I would remember."

I told her about hiring a private investigator that said my mother's name was Marilyn Hanson. "It's strange that he had your first name and birthday correct. But that's behind me now. I'm ecstatic to have found you well and thriving. I showed your picture to a close friend and she said you look half your age."

"Aww," she said, "thank you, honey. I don't know why, because I spent my life living on the beach. It's a wonder I'm not all wrinkled up."

We left our first meal together in good humor, joking with each other all the way home. The moon was almost full, and as we turned into her gated community, it shone on the sign at the entrance. It was the symbol of her community ... a white bird in flight.

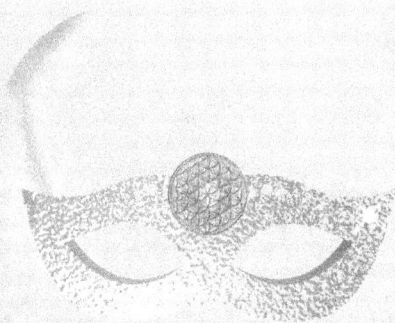

PART 5
MASQUERADE

27

UNDERCOVER MEETINGS

I figured out my highest ancestry match listed as A.K. was my mother's only niece, Anita Kavalier. How she didn't recognize A.K.'s initials is beyond me.

I contacted Anita through her daughter-in-law, Dawn Finger, who had the exact same name as the Dawn I traveled to Naples to find. Both Dawns had Kavalier names in their Facebook friends. That uncanny coincidence took me on a wild goose chase to Florida when the real A.K. lived in Washington State.

Anita had no idea that my uncle Henson was her father when she was growing up. She was lied to as a child because her mother loathed him. Her mother married again and told Anita the new husband was her father. When Anita was seven, Henson came knocking on her door and told her, "I'm your father." That was the first and last time she saw him because her mother chased him out of the house with a butcher knife.

I hoped to find out more because M&M said her brother and my father were best friends. Anita didn't have anything to go on, but she did fill me in on some interesting tidbits. Two of the women in our family were psychics. They held seances and read palms and tarot cards on Redondo Beach. I was betting they were the ones the psychic in Cassadaga made contact with.

When I told M&M and Macy who A.K. was, they remembered Anita, but neither had spoken with her for years. I tried contacting my uncle's other wives and their families to see if anyone knew who his best friend had been. That had me spinning my wheels for months.

I solved the A.K. mystery but was far from finding the man whose genes I carry.

By Chance

I booked a ticket to Costa Rica to get some dental work done. Driving to Miami to catch the flight, I stopped by to see M&M. On arrival, she was on a phone call with her grandson Chris. He was in Costa Rica fishing, and she told him I was going down and passed the phone to me. We briefly chatted, with Chris thinking I was just a friend.

My dental work only took a few days, then I rented a car and headed to the Pacific for a dose of ocean breeze. On the way, I passed a sign with the name of the place Chris said he was staying. Turning around, I drove into the gravel driveway and asked someone which house Chris lived in. He was two doors down and had just come in from fishing. I called out his name, and he came out. I told him I just saw the sign and thought to say hi. His wife and daughter then came out, and I got to take photos. The resemblance of their daughter to me when I was her age astonished me.

When I hit the States, I called MM and told her about the chance meeting. She seemed delighted and had no qualms about it. I told her again it would mean so much to know who my father was. She said she'd tell me but didn't remember his name.

I had a bit of pouting drama going on, and I think she felt guilty. To cheer me up, she surprised me by agreeing to let me meet "her family" on my next visit. The condition was I had to keep my identity under wraps. I'd do just about anything to meet them in person, no matter how wrong being a secret was.

Posing as a Photographer

M&M planned a party inviting family and her close friends. Besides being able to meet my family, I'd get photos because I was deemed the party photographer! Our story was that my mother had been one of her best friends. That wasn't really a lie. Within a few minutes, after people arrived, she blew it by saying I was a friend who used to live in the area. I was already in shock trying to act normal, and that put me on the edge of a breakdown. For the next eternity of an afternoon, I witnessed myself as an actress improvising at every moment.

When my half-sister, Deanna, came in, she approached me and asked how we were related. I looked to Macy to see if she'd spilled the beans but got no response. "Deanna," I said, "My mother was close friends with your mother when she lived in Miami." That seemed to suffice. Macy told me later that Deanna always asked such things when meeting someone new. That was weird, but I believed her at the time.

Nic came late and was standoffish. At one point, Deanna was standing in front of a blank white wall, and I asked Nic if he'd stand next to his sister for a photo. He said, "I don't like people telling me what to do." His wife, Brenda, was friendlier and said they were going to a party and invited me to go with them. I bowed out, but when they left early, my emotions unexpectedly erupted. Excusing myself, I rushed out back and laid low. Sobbing into the ground, I grabbed onto the grass, trying to hold myself together.

The party was petering out when I returned. After everyone left, M&M talked on and on about her family, everybody but me, that is. I don't think she even missed me when I left the party. It seemed fruitless to share my grief.

Nic called, as usual, every night. I always walked outside to give her privacy, but this night I overheard her saying, "Oh, she left, don't worry about me." She lied with such convincing authoritarian ease that I knew it was habitual.

Over the next few days, we went through her photo albums. I took pics of them and jotted down notes as she told me about each one. I think all the memories got her brain syntax working at high speed. Before I left, she told me my father's name.

With a name like Fabian Naberry, it'd be easy to track him down. Right? After days of searching, however, I was still in a fog. There were no matches, and MM didn't recognize any of the surnames in my three DNA test results. Then I found one long shot and made contact. We talked a few times, and it looked like his brother, who had passed, might be my father since he was in Redondo Beach, California, the year of my conception. In the month we waited for his DNA test results, I began calling him Uncle. But it turned out that we weren't related at all. Coming out of that rabbit hole left me lifeless.

Back to India

I sorely missed my spiritual father and took off for two months to India. It was Gurudev's sanyas birthday, and a big celebration was happening in Haridwar. I fell back into singing and being with him as much as possible between the thrones of devotees vying for his attention. After Haridwar, it was easier to have private time with him as we traveled to a remote village where he'd built the first ashram.

I told Gurudev about my biological findings showing him pictures of my mother. When I asked if he could tell me about my biological father, he said to remember this life is like a dream, analogous to optical images on a movie screen, and that I should look at the light of the projector. He said I'd have a better chance of understanding the truth if I visualized the universe as a mere dream.

Before leaving India, Gurudev said I'd know who my father was when the time was right. That was the third time I'd heard that. Once was from a psychic, and the other was from the Brighu reading. But that didn't deter me from the search.

April Fool's Day

It was Easter 2018 and April Fool's Day to boot, so I played a trick on M&M. Calling to wish her a Happy Easter, I told her I found my father, and he was heavenly handsome and wanted to meet her again. She got all fired up. "Who is he? What's his name? Where does he live?" Her anxious response told me my father could very well be someone else. I said it was my turn to ask questions. "Do you want to meet him?" She kept asking for more details which I elusively answered. In the end, she agreed to meet him and was super excited about it. I ended the call by saying, "It's a good thing today's April Fool's Day."

A month later, I drove down to spend Mother's Day with M&M after the rest of her family had left. I brought her an invitation to my first birthday party coming up on Summer Solstice. It was an important event to celebrate finding her and a delicious delight for the kid in me. Of course, she wouldn't dare come, but she had fun hearing all the plans.

My friends, family, and Angel were all coming dressed as kids. I planned prizes and games like hula hoop contests, pinata bashing, potato bag races, tire swinging, and pin the tail on the president. My band, The Tameless, would play two sets, and I'd sing and tap dance. There'd be a welcome station to sign in for prizes as they sat down on whoopee cushions. Face paint, hair glitter, and costumes were collected, and I'd already made a big banner for the adult lemonade stand. My friend Steve was to dress up like the Good Humor Man to serve ice cream, and another friend was dressing as a famous chef to cook in my solar oven. I'd made homemade peanut butter and assorted jams and had all my favorite kid foods ready. M&M couldn't stop giggling and made me promise to bring her party pictures.

Original Birth Certificate

She asked what I'd like for my birthday, and I told her the best gift would be to get my original birth certificate. I'd already printed out the necessary papers to send to Florida Vital Statistics. She agreed to sign them, and I drove us to the nearby shipping store and got her signature notarized. The documents immediately went off by certified mail.

On the way home, we stopped at a drugstore to pick up a blood test since she didn't know what type she was. I was betting on her being O-negative. The pharmacy was out of tests, but they had a sale on 23andMe DNA kits. It didn't take a minute for me to grab one. I got her saliva in a tube that night and sent it off.

Maybe some other siblings from another lover she had would show up. If so, it could make finding my father an easier undertaking. I asked more about her first husband and when they got divorced. She didn't remember but said it was in Vegas, and she had a record of it.

We hunted for her divorce papers for over two hours before giving up. I guess it's true, "What happens in Vegas, stays in Vegas."

28

THE GAMBLE

My first birthday party was outrageously fun. Seeing my adult friends dressed as kids in knickers and baby doll dresses was hysterical. Just before sunset, my friend Julia brought over her white doves and released them to honor my newfound freedom from secrecy. Then she handed me a basket with one final dove. I opened it, and the bird flew up, following the others, soaring westward and circling back above me. Julia said my white bird, like me, traveled unusual airwaves.

After the party extravaganza, I drove back to see M&M in Florida to show her photos and videos from my party. Picking up my mail on the way out, I found a letter from Florida Vital Statistics saying they received the information to issue my birth certificate. But, the big but was my mother's notarized name, Kavalier, didn't match the last name on my original birth certificate.

I drove straight through. My old car acted as pissed and confused as I was, rattling all the way. Stopping for gas, I reread the letter. "This is not your mother's name." I said it over and over again in disbelief. By the time I got to her house, I'd composed an entire song around it.

Showing M&M the letter, I asked for an explanation. She changed the subject a few times and then said she thought the state must have made a mistake. With that, I hit the sack.

She was up early, and to cheer me up, she took me to our favorite oceanside breakfast spot. Looking away from her out at the vast waters, it hit me. My adoption papers stated I was Infant Hanson. I made a gamble and bet M&M a hundred bucks that she used that name. She was sure she hadn't and took me on. To prove who the winner was, she had to sign another notarized document. This time she'd have to lie and state her name was Marilyn Hanson. On the way home, we stopped at the same shipping store where they knew her. She signed with no identification, and I sent the document off by overnight express.

I won the gamble! But I'm still waiting for my $100.

Paternal Findings

Two months later, the brick wall came tumbling down when I got a paternal first-cousin match. My eyes were still bulging when I called Angel with the exciting news. She got right on it and sent me 13 pages of information about my match.

Her name was Eva, and she was three years older than me. Eva and I shared over 2,000 centimorgans of DNA, which meant she might even be a half-sister. That was confusing because her last name was not listed as a surname in any of my DNA results, nor was it the surname my mother gave me.

She'd been married a few times and had nine alias names. Looking further, I found 39 other relatives listed; two were men with the same name my mother gave me, Fabian Naberry. One was my age, and the other was 96. If one was my father, then why didn't his surname of Naberry show DNA results? And even if the younger one was his son, it didn't make sense that I'd have a brother my same age. Trapped inside the enigma, scenarios buzzed around me like hornets trying to escape.

Angel nudged me to take action by unearthing 11 related phone numbers and 12 different addresses, all in Nevada. Jittering with the phone in hand, I began calling. After reaching numerous disconnected numbers, I got an answering machine. It was a man's voice. I left a message with my name, saying I was trying to reach Eva.

Researching the number further, I discovered he lived at Eva's latest address. Property records showed them both listed as owners of that address. He was 13 years younger than her, so it couldn't be her son.

I called the next day again, and he answered. When I told him I was trying to reach Eva, he said, "Your name is Valerie Edra Naiman, and you're in North Carolina." Yes, I squealed, excited that he knew who I was. Demandingly he asked, "But who are you?" I told him I believed Eva was my cousin, aunt, or half-sister because we shared matching DNA to confirm that. He interrogated me for about an hour with a slew of questions. By the time we hung up, I knew for sure that Eva was my half-sister and he was her husband, Wade.

Implying he was a big deal, Wade said if I knew who he was, I'd understand the reason for his extreme cautiousness. He had "his people" working on finding out more about me. If I checked out, then he'd get back to me.

Angel and I researched through the night and discovered the younger male was Eva's brother. All signs pointed to me having a brother only three months younger than me.

Wade called the next day and said he knew I wasn't a terrorist or assassin. "I don't think it's in my genes." I said. In the meantime, I'd already found criminal records on him and was concerned for Eva. I carefully asked him about it, and he said I must have been looking for someone else because that wasn't him.

He had pictures of Eva and me taken when we were about the same age and was astounded. Our similarities were undeniable. My serotonin skyrocketed at the thought of seeing my features in another human. When I asked how Eva was doing physically, he laughed and said she was in excellent health. Then he jolted me with a shock treatment that went clear through my bones.

"Eva knows exactly who your mother is!"

My inner community went berserk. M&M said she didn't know any of his family! How could she have kept this from me? I already knew my mother gave the bogus name of Hanson on my birth records and had concocted a profile of herself as never having been married and me being her first child, so why should I be surprised?

I was reeling when Wade said he felt safe for me to connect with Eva, but it was up to her whether she wanted to talk to me or not.

Who Was My Father?

Speaking to my sister for the first time was monumental. Eva was communicative and warm as she burned through my illusions. Scads of my mother's lies rose to the surface in the next few hours. Eva said she'd known my mother very well ever since she was a kid. She had pictures of my parents together taken years after my birth! The story was that my mother was a friend of the family. Trust in my mother sunk like jewels on the Titanic.

Eva said our father was handsomely flamboyant and treated her like a princess. He was a ladies' man and had gone through numerous relationships and marriages. She said he went to Miami often when she was a kid, and my mother repeatedly visited them when they moved to Vegas. In our father's last days, none of the family had seen my mother. Our father, along with decades of secrets, was buried in Vegas in 2003.

Eva thought he didn't marry my mother because her mom got pregnant, and he felt obligated to stay with her. She said her brother believed that's why Dad treated him badly. Even so, my newfound brother, Fabian Jr., wanted to meet me. His nickname was Fabe.

The reason Eva took the DNA test was to find out who our grandmother was. Her own mother spent years trying to find out because our father never knew who his real mother was. Dad was two when he was renamed Fabian Naberry. He found out 15 years later that he was adopted.

No wonder I hadn't been able to match up a surname. My father was named after his original father, Franklin Heath Cobb, Jr., who left a wild trail to follow. Our grandfather was a producer who owned theaters in Chicago and Hollywood. He directed and produced musicals there as well as in NYC. Eva had numerous archives about him and said he was a big womanizer and had been in multiple relationships. He married five times, and once it was two marriages at the same time. It was a case of like father, like son.

Eva still didn't know who our grandmother was. She had a copy of our father's birth certificate that stated his mother's name was Robert Wayne Turner. How could a birth certificate show a man's name for a baby's mother? No doubt, it was a coverup for somebody. The handwritten certificate also stated the birth was not legitimate. Well, that must make me an illegitimate child of an illegitimate child. That makes me a big ole double negative. But since I'm a double negative, doesn't that make me positive? All my inner community characters consented and gave me a thumbs up.

There was an actress back in vaudeville named Edith Teleofaro, and Eva said that our father was born in her Chicago home in 1922. Teleofaro was rumored to be our grandmother's best friend. Researching, we discovered she played the lead in a 1915 silent Paramount Picture movie called *Young Romance*. But after tons of research, I still hadn't unmasked the mystery of my grandmother.

I invited Eva to come to visit me in Asheville. She wasn't into traveling but welcomed me to come to Vegas. The closest airport wasn't far from her house, and I didn't waste time booking a flight.

First Contact with Brother

Brother Fabe was excited to talk to me and wondered if his father was really his father. "So, we have the same Dad," he said, "that's amazing and weird." He hadn't known about me, but he sure knew my mother and her brother, Henson Kavalier. Our father, he said, went to Union High School with them.

All these years, he thought my mother was a family friend who'd been Dad's crush back in the day. Dad was married to his mom when my life was seeded, and I suspected my mother was married throughout the decades of trumped-up alibis. Fabe said his mother must have known and just put up with it. He wished we could have had a relationship all these years.

Fabe and I both grew up in the 60s and connected with ease. He fought in Vietnam while I protested the war. We were both musicians and had oodles of stories to share.

Fabe had already put together a big box of photos to show me as soon as I got there. He found me online and showed his friends pictures of his new sister. He asked if I was a Buddhist because he'd seen pictures of me in India. I told him I ran the religious gamut and ended up believing our lives were imposed mystical dramas from our karma. That cracked him up, and he said I must have gotten my entertainment genes from our grandfather."

We ended by saying we already loved each other.

Vegas

Eva picked me up at the airport, but instead of going to her house, she took me to the Strip so I'd experience Vegas. I only wanted to meet the family and told her that seeing Vegas wasn't important. She insisted, saying they'd already booked my room at one of their places.

She dropped me off at Caesars Palace with a plan to pick me up the next day to go to her house for a family gathering. I dropped my bag at the front desk and walked through the noisy casino, which led to another casino and another. Wandering lost through a windowless maze of bright lights, flashing ding-a-ling-games, poker rooms, and hundreds of shops, I ended up in an indoor shopping mall underneath a big fake sky. I felt more like Moses in the bible than an opulent roman empress. My attire was far from Vegasy. I might as well have been an alien wearing a stranger in a strange land billboard.

I got to my room and tried to cozy up in the enormous space. No number of pillows and comforters were enough to protect my raw cold vulnerability, but at least it was quiet.

In the morning, I came down 20-plus flights and waited in the lobby amidst the early cha-ching-a-lings bouncing through the airwaves. This had been my sister's daily environment when she was a prominent Vegas card dealer. I tried my luck at a slot machine and won on my third spin. That was enough gambling for me.

Eva picked me up, and off we went to her home. My brother, Fabe, welcomed me with a big long hug, and Shannon, my sister's son, and his wife, Connie, along with Eva's husband, Wade, were all there. We hung out in the kitchen while Eva spread photos across a large serve-through counter. I took pictures and made notes of who was who. My exuberance must have been too much for Wade, and he settled himself into a lazy boy in the next room.

Fabe had a mother-lode of old family photos of our father. I flipped when he brought out pictures of my birth parents together. The queen of deception was royally exposed. Besides the lovey-dovey pictures of them taken years after my birth, one in particular threw me for a loop. They were standing together, holding a foot-long stick horizontally between them. Both my parents were smiling at a bird sitting on the stick. A white cockatoo with blue eyes.

Wade got Eva on her ancestry site and showed me the family trees they'd made that had about a thousand people in them. We exchanged account passwords, thinking I could pick up the ball and find answers to the remaining grandmother mystery.

After lunch, Wade's mood changed when Eva went to the other room for something. He remarked that some people didn't want me there prying into their lives. Eva overheard some of this and asked him to stop. The anger in the room turned into bickering, and I was soon a vulnerable mess. My chest of joy collapsed into fight or flight. Feeling awkwardly unwanted, I told Eva it was probably time for me to go to the hotel.

Driving me back to the palace, Eva apologized for Wade's behavior. Trying to comfort me, she said he was the one that was uncomfortable with me being there, not her or her son or my brother. She felt terrible about the scene and said she'd return in the morning for us to go shopping. It was all I could do not to break down.

Wade's episode had hit an artery triggering my abandonment issues all over again. There's no way I'd stay at Ceasar's if it was on his dime. I didn't know if Eva or her husband was the high roller, but I was out of there. I checked out and moved to the LINQ hotel across the street. When Eva returned, I met her in front of Caesars, and off we went shopping away the day. Neither of us mentioned what had happened. I felt safe being with her, and I didn't care what we did as long as we were together. I had a sister, and all I wanted to do was deepen our bond.

Topping off the day, Fabe joined us for dinner and a Cirque du Soleil performance at the Mirage on the Strip. Eva spent most of the show looking at her phone and then disappeared. I imagined Wade was bugging her. What was up with him? Did he think I was after their money? I didn't understand, but I was sure glad I got to Vegas as soon as I did, or I may have never met Eva and Fabe.

After the show, we found Eva drinking in the lobby. It troubled me to see her so disengaged. It took all my strength to not take it personally. I told myself it was my test to stay centered and drum up compassion for both of us.

Fabe invited me to visit the Valley of Fire the next day. Eva said she couldn't go but encouraged me to. I thought it was a Wade thing and hoped she'd work out whatever the real issue was. Fabe was a boon of kindheartedness and continued to lift my spirits. He picked me up, and we spent an incredible day checking out petroglyphs, taking selfies against the sandstone peaks, and deepening our relationship.

That night lying in bed looking out at a humongous Ferris wheel, I felt like I'd come full circle on a lifetime journey.

His Way

I woke up to a text from Eva saying she and Wade were leaving for their beach house for a few days. Hoping for an invitation, even if Wade was involved, I replied that it sounded fun and I loved getting my toes in the sand. After an hour of not hearing more from Eva, I called Fabian and shared my disappointment. I invited him to come for a spa treatment and lunch. He said he'd pick me up, and we'd go on an adventure instead. He also said I should check out of my hotel and stay with him for a few days. Following his lead, I did just that.

We had a jamming music session at his place, cooked up a storm, and swapped stories until midnight. That was the kind of adventure I needed. The next day we gathered flowers and traveled to our father's gravesite. Burning sage, I smudged our way through rows of markers until I stood six feet above my father. There were so many questions I wanted to ask ... so much I wanted to say. I never knew if he ever held me, looked for me, or loved me. I deserved more than this bittersweet ending.

Addressing him by his birth name, Franklin Heath Cobb, Jr., I let years of tears cascade down upon his tombstone. There was nothing to say and nothing more I could do. After my intense release, my breathing deepened, and everything quieted down. A sense of peace enveloped me. Leaving my long search to rest, I beseeched his soul to keep me posted on his karmic outcome. Who knew what was next?

His tombstone was chiseled with five words summing up his life. "I Did It My Way."

Fabe and I went to a secluded pool to chill out after my emotional landslide. Setting my phone down to pull a snorkel over my head, a text from Eva popped up.

"We've been fighting ever since you arrived and it would be better if you were gone when we returned."

There went my calm state. I was about to go off the deep end again. I turned away from Fabe, pulling my mask down over a private numbing pain until fog was all there was.

When Fabe found out what happened, there wasn't much to say. He took me for ice cream, and we sat in silence. That night we went to the top of the tallest building in Vegas, overlooking the vast madness of lights spread out in grids in every direction. The view mirrored the maze of my long, bizarre search.

On my return flight, I committed to compiling this book. I'd come to the end of my search, but there was still the mystery of who my grandmother was. Opening my computer at a stopover, I tried logging into Eva's family tree. The passcode didn't work. I called and emailed Eva to see if she'd changed it but got no response. I knew the passcode worked when I was there. Not only that, but her public tree was now private, and I was blocked from seeing anything. I left messages for Fabe and didn't hear from him either. Damn it, why didn't I print the whole thing out when I was in Vegas

Despite reaching out many times, I never heard from Eva again and didn't hear from Fabe for three years.

29

HE COULDN'T DANCE

Regrouping at home for a week, I audio-recorded some of my stories and burned them on a CD for MM. I bought a player and couldn't resist making a slideshow of the telltale photos from Vegas with the keepsake song from my father's epitaph. Then I headed to Florida to confront my mother.

I played it cool, and we hugged and then snuggled up on her couch. First, I let her go on about what was happening with 'her family.' Then I begged her to tell me about my father. She looked out at the lake and drifted off into her own world. I'll never forget the gentle smile on her face when she said, "He was special. You know, he would have given anything to see you. If only he could be with us now."

I told her she was in for a surprise and to sit at the kitchen table. I set up my computer, cued up the show, and popped in the CD. I let "My Way" play through once first. She looked at the player with a fixed gaze, putting on her glasses to see it better. Then I turned her to face the slideshow. She moved closer to the screen in disbelief when the song began again. I softly sang along ... "And now the end is near, and so I face the final curtain." Their love was not only obvious in the photos but in her sighs. The last photo was a closeup of my father's tombstone. Lost in memories she had denied, she gently ran her finger over my computer screen.

Their secret love affair and shenanigans had gone on for decades. At 96, her memory was fine, except for intentionally blocking her clandestine escapades. Keeping my father and me a secret for most of her life showed in the lines on her face. However, the video unearthed treasured memories, and her whole demeanor softened. Within minutes, she looked years younger. For me, I felt an enormous weight lift. Knowing I was a love child and not a one-night stand lifted my spirits. That was way better than being an illegitimate bastard.

M&M wanted to hear everything I'd discovered. I told her about the Las Vegas trip, and we talked through the night. When I played some of my audio recordings from Vegas, she made me promise to send her more. I told her I would make an audiobook about my search.

We slept in late and picked up where we'd left off. MM wanted to see the slideshow again, and I set it on repeat while I packed up. I asked her why she didn't marry him when he proposed. Not only did he love her, but he was a knockout good-looker. He had a successful construction business, a boat, and an airplane. Was it that she was already married? She didn't answer that, but she went on about how he loved her way too much. Then she leaned closer to me and whispered, "Ya know honey ... he couldn't dance."

30

STUFFED LOVE

Back home, I began a search for my grandmother. I was devastated to still not be able to open Eva's ancestry tree. I called, texted, and emailed again to see if she had changed the password. No response ever came. I guess chump was written across my forehead when we exchanged passcodes. And then, it got worse. I went to my account and found that the extensive family trees I'd worked on for years had vanished. Years of work ... sabotaged. I continued to try and contact Eva and Fabe numerous times over the next few years.

I made some more audio recordings of my experience while it was still fresh in my mind and burned them into a CD. After Thanksgiving in 2019, I packed some gifts and the CD and drove south to see MM again. I planned to stay a week but left after one day.

It was all about a stuffed monkey she had. When I got there, a stuffed monkey was sitting on her table in the kitchen. I picked it up and it said, "I love you." I really wanted that monkey as a keepsake and asked if I could have it. "Oh no," she said, "A friend gave that to me." I asked her what friend but she didn't remember. How could it be so important if she didn't even know who gifted it to her?

I'd always spoiled her with gifts, and the absolute "no" triggered me big time. She'd already listened to the first audio CD I gave her and knew about the monkey story of my birth. Crushed, I told her I needed some sleep after the long drive and went to nurse my wounds in private.

In the morning, seeing the monkey again made it worse. I made a pot of coffee, filled my thermos, and left abruptly, telling MM I had to go see Jodee.

Driving to Miami, I pressed my palm to my heart to stop the erratic pounding. I don't know what a heart attack feels like, but it scared me. Was it a fear of a double whammy rejection? Or was I a pouting brat because I didn't get my way? I tried to remind myself I was a grown-up senior citizen, but that didn't help.

I was a mess when I got to Miami and spent the next few days spilling it out with Jodee. The incident was so silly, but it engulfed me. Talking it through with her and calling Angel Mary helped me understand the adoptee quagmire I'd sunken into. The love monkey grenade re-sparked early trauma and opened a deep wound. Angel said it's the kind of adoptee trauma that lies dormant until provoked. I worked through it until I felt stable enough to return to MM's. The rest of the week with my mother was full of sharing and laughter.

DNA Surprise

Macy came, and unbeknownst to me, she'd gotten a DNA test. I thought she did it because she was still unsure about me. She said my DNA didn't match up with hers. Looking into it, I found not only did she not share DNA with me but she didn't have a trace of it with my mother. That explained another mystery of why her son, Parker, didn't match my DNA. He'd created a tree based on what he was told, not through a test. Macy and Parker's mistaken identities had blazed the trail leading me to my mother.

I told her I'd help her find out the truth and that she might be writing a book about her mystery too. She was shocked, angry, and scared someone would find out. Macy had me vow not to tell my mother. How many secrets could I hold in?

Before leaving, I told MM if she passed away before me that I wanted her love monkey. She agreed, and we wrote a note that she safety pinned to the monkey's back, saying, "I belong to Valerie." I reminded her that if I passed first, my sign for her to know my Soul was thrivingly alive would be a white feather. She responded that hers would be a red rose.

On the drive back to Asheville, I saw the exit to Cassadaga and swerved off. Maybe I could get a hit from a psychic on my grandmother's name. I pulled up to the metaphysical shop and recognized a woman I'd met before. She was the one that referred me to a psychic to find my mother. Asking her if a reader was on site, she informed me that she was. As we entered a private room she said, "I remember you were looking for your mother's name." Yes," I said, "I finally found her and" … Interrupting me she said, "I see red roses and get the name Rose."

31

THE RED ROSE

Separation ensued as Covid hit in March 2020. We talked often, and one day MM drove out for groceries and crashed into another vehicle. She was unscathed but ended up in the hospital for a few days. Back home, she was still sore, especially her back. I was able to maneuver getting her on medical marijuana, which alleviated some of her pain. At least she was able to gallivant around in her new golf cart.

I kept clean so I could see her when the pandemic lifted. The worst part was not having a hug in months. At least being a mama to goats I could hug my two kids. When there was no cream in the stores, I decided to get Nigerian dwarf goats and they've been such a delight. Who'da thought I'd have kids at 69? With still no end in sight for the masked distancing dance, my life was gardening, taking care of farm animals, and writing.

MM and I kept up with each other a few times a week. She was always chipper and talkative. We thought the pandemic would end soon but months passed as covid escalated. Playing out the secret masquerade became more challenging as the mandated separation triggered infant wounds.

One day, Macy texted me that my mother had a stroke and was hospitalized for two days. Despite covid, I packed up thinking I'd be her caregiver. I called and found out Deanna had already hired one, and MM was on the way home in an ambulance. A therapist would be helping her get stable on her feet again.

I spoke to MM that night to let her know I'd be there asap. She said her physical therapist was helping her so we could go dancing again. As I was leaving the next morning, Macy messaged me that MM's therapist tested positive for covid. They were all in quarantine.

I kept my bags packed, ready to go down when ten days of quarantine were over. I called again that night, and the caregiver answered saying she didn't want to disturb MM because she was resting and hadn't been eating. I told her to try ice cream because MM loved it so much. I asked her to tell MM I wasn't coming because of their quarantine.

The caregiver was shocked and asked how I knew that since it was only information shared with the family. I sashayed around the question, and when we hung up, I got a call from my secret brother, Nic. I was too nervous to answer. He called numerous times asking me to return his call.

When I told Macy she emphatically said he was mean and I'd better not reply. I'd only met him that one time at MM's party, where I posed as a photographer. It didn't make any sense that he was calling. The caregiver must have suspected something and given him my number.

Being undercover, I couldn't penetrate the barrier while honoring my mother's secret. After chewing my split ends for two days, I called MM. She answered herself and her voice was unusually soft, but she was very coherent. I asked what she wanted for Christmas, and she said she only wanted to see me. 'Her' family was coming for the holidays, and she said it was best to come on the 27th so we'd have more time together.

I put together a box of fun gifts for her and sent it by express mail. When I called few days later, the caregiver said MM was sleeping and not doing well. I asked if my gift package came and she said no one had seen it. Following up, I called the next day, and the caregiver passed the phone to my mother. MM always got a kick out of hearing her nickname when I called. "Hi M&M, are you feeling any better? Did you get my surprise box?" She rambunctiously hollered out, "It's my daughter!"

I reminded her I was supposed to be a secret and to my utter delight, she said, "There are no secrets anymore." I wanted to bust out of my Clark Kent persona and fly to her side. I'll come right away, I said. She laughed, saying she wasn't having much fun without me. Since her family was on the way, she thought it was best to come after Christmas as planned so we'd have more time together.

I called Macy and told her the good news of not being a secret anymore. She furiously lit into me, yelling that my mother wasn't in her right mind and not to listen to her. Macy's tone was a 180 turnaround. In her frenzied rant, she said I had to remain a secret and not come to Florida. She hung up as my Superman high skidded to the ground.

The first snow fell as temperatures dropped to the lowest in history on Christmas Eve in Asheville. It was a quiet night, as everyone in the community had left on vacation. Packing up a few last-minute things to take to MM, I kept hearing her voice saying there were no secrets anymore. Macy's demand was not my mother's. I'd wait until their family get-together, but the cover-ups were over. I fired up the woodstove and settled in to write. The muse was with me as I wrote non-stop until the wee hours of the morning.

I awoke to find a thick white blanket covering the landscape. When I was able to pry my deck door open and step outside, my ankle boots were totally submerged in the snow. Only an inch was called for, but we got seven. I spent most of Christmas with pen in hand only stopping to feed the fire and goats.

Connection Beyond Grief

Macy called, and for the first time, I dreaded answering the phone.

My mother passed away Christmas night.

~❖~

I lit a candle by her framed photograph and stared into the flame as memories swept over me in waves. Grief broke me down until I couldn't feel anything. Closing my eyes, I began deep breathing to bring life back into me. After a while, it was gratefulness that flowed back out through my tears. Then every inhale began to smell like roses. At first, I thought it was the frankincense I had burned the night before but the essence intensified with each breath. There was no doubt it was roses.

I felt my mother's presence envelop me and then it was like she was smiling through me. Words fail to portray the incredible experience of the unconditional love I felt. I have no idea how long this timeless reunion lasted.

When I finally opened my eyes, they landed directly on a gift that I had bought for my mother. I had taken it out of the overstuffed Christmas box I shipped to her because it didn't fit in. I thought it wouldn't be useful anyway since it was a shopping bag and she wasn't going out much. The bag folds into itself, creating a flower. That flower is a rose and is now profoundly precious to me.

My mother had said if she left this world before me that she would send me a sign from the other side. That way I'd know she was fine and her Soul was alive. I was staring at her sign ... a beautiful red rose.

The Divine's mysterious ways of speaking never ceases to amaze me. Since my mother passed, I've been doing fire rituals for her ongoing journey. A white feather balances on top of her red rose, nurturing my loss. If only I had just gone during covid. If only I hadn't been a secret. But I had to believe everything was in divine order. I'd go to her memorial and hopefully have a reunion with my siblings.

Rejection

I called, texted, and emailed my half-sister, Deanna, giving my condolences. Hoping she'd remember me, I sent a photo I took of her with MM. I said I always loved that picture I took at the party when we met. I asked if I could help in any way and said I'd be coming to the memorial. She never responded.

Macy called saying only immediate family could come. Deanna must have told her I said I was coming. I was more immediate than Macy but she said now was a terrible time to break the news because everyone was grieving. Only a few hours later, she texted saying the memorial had already happened at MM's bedside just before she passed. Macy wasn't even there because it was so impromptu.

I called Macy and didn't recognize her voice. I'd never heard her speak so callously before. With icy disdain, she asked why I'd even want to go. They already sent my mother's body to the crematorium and there wouldn't even be a corpse to see. Sickened by her harsh words, I couldn't reply. Grief smothered me, bringing my breath to a slow moan as I laid down paralyzed by the fire.

32

THE NATURE OF KIN

Macy's cantankerous insensitivity tormented my core. How could I have let her be my trusted confidant? It made no sense that Mother's passing, memorial, and cremation had already happened. Triggers skyrocketed, propelled by fierce anger until I exhausted myself into a debilitated wreck.

I asked Macy to rescue my love monkey. She said they'd already cleared out M&M's house to sell it and she didn't see it. Nic had taken stuff to thrift stores, and she and Deanna would go there and look for it. She said Deanna gave her a suitcase of some things that she knew were mine. What? Deanna knew who I was?

Macy spewed out a flimsy story that Deanna had her mother's DNA tested. She said she got MM's saliva when taking her to the dentist. That's impossible BS! Then Macy's story changed saying MM's grandchildren got her a DNA test for Christmas a few years ago and that's how Deanna knew.

A few years ago?! That slapped my brains out. In one deep gulp, the confidence I had in Macy plummeted. My inner community was screaming one after another. "You're a total nincompoop!" ... "I told you never to trust anyone" ... "She tricked your dumb ass!" Macy must have told my sister to begin with and played me for a fool. Betrayal sent me running for my bed fort.

Macy said Deanna's known for quite a while and was not interested in connecting with me. Rejection laced with betrayal was more than I could handle. Struck down, I wrapped my arms around me like a straight jacket. No one could get to me now, not even myself.

It took days to come out of shock and let myself think again. I texted Macy that since she wasn't blood-related that Deanna must know her secret. Macy never contacted me again.

Breakthrough

Outcast and alone, there was nothing to keep me from calling my brother Nic. Ripped raw, I figured it was easier to take on another blow while I was down for the count.

Nic answered and when I told him my name, he said he knew exactly who I was. The morning after our mother passed, Deanna had told him offhandedly. He said he was always the last to know anything. We both had been duped.

Nic was kind and open, not mean like Macy said. He called me sister and said he wished he could have known me all along. I found out Deanna and Macy never went looking for my monkey but they asked him to. He spent hours rummaging through the thrift stores but never found it. I asked if he saw the CDs and boombox I got MM. It humored him to find out I'd gotten the player because Deanna told him she did. The more we talked, the more my hoodwinked brain cleared up.

He said if Macy knew who I was, then Deanna knew all along because they were hitched like velcro. Right after I first met MM on that indelible Halloween, our mother's last wishes were changed without him knowing it. Somehow the peas in a pod upped their ante and demoted Nic. The timing made me believe that they thought I was a threat to their inheritance. That also explained why Macy didn't want anyone to know her secret of not being related to the family. Nic and I talked for over an hour and we've been talking or texting every week since.

Despite not having a relationship with my two sisters, I have a wonderful connection with my two brothers. I went to Florida and had a reunion with Nic. Then out of the blue, my paternal brother Robbie from Vegas came with his daughter to visit me in Asheville. He apologized for not responding to me for all these years. He'd been in the hospital on his deathbed and had moved in with his daughter. Meeting my niece for the first time was worth the wait.

Having the love of both my brothers was a big surprise since I always thought sisters would be the ones to open their arms and embrace me. With my illusions shattered, I finally was able to move out of the fog.

My new bumper sticker reads - Question Assumptions!

In James Sherman's book, *Rejection*, he urges us not to fixate on the past. He said, "You can't go back and make a new start, but you can start right now and make a brand new ending."

Having never subscribed to the can't word, my perspective is that we can indeed change our feelings about the past by how we perceive it. In effect then, we can change our past and create a new story. We can do that and turn our trauma into a conscious tool for our own evolution.

33
SWAN SONG

The falling snow is whisking in the gusty winds tonight, mimicking thoughts about my whirlwind search. Was it worth it? To answer that question, I need to know what is valuable and prioritize what's most vital to me. Food, shelter, and water are the physical basics, but what about my mental, emotional, and spiritual being?

I need to have it all in balance. One of my heroes is the author and scientist Dr. Masaru Emoto. He proved that sound and intention affect the molecular structure of water. If you project negative thoughts on water, chaotic ugly structural patterns form, but exquisite formations appear when projecting positive thoughts. He calls it fractal enlightenment.

Quantum physics has proven that our thoughts manipulate particles and create our reality. Positive thoughts result in positive outcomes, while negative ones do the opposite. Because of that, I refuse to believe I am a victim. That would mean I don't have power over my life. I firmly believe we can alter our lives with thought and intention. We can use this skill to benefit ourselves, others, and the world around us.

This is not some new age woo-woo espousing. As Einstein said, "Imagination is more important than knowledge."

Was the enormous energy I spent on my search worth it? Could I have used it for something more important? I do know that the journey enriched me with the most valuable lessons of my life. It was much more than a ransack into my genealogy. It was a search for divine truth.

Had I not had the deep desire to find my roots, I might have missed numerous opportunities for personal growth. I ended the search with an understanding that my adoptee trauma was a gift that kick-started me to find my authentic self. In some way, I have outfoxed karma.

Beyond any doubt, the long search was worth it! It changed my inner dialogue, beliefs, and values.

I changed my story. I changed my life.

DEDICATION

For my father, Jules, who gave me my first manual typewriter and encouraged me to write. And to Klea, my mother, who taught me how to manifest my dreams. And to my incredible teachers, family, friends, and inspiring adoptee tribe that believed in me and supported the creation of this book. If I list everyone by name, this book will be as fat as Steinbeck's *Grapes of Wrath*. Besides, I'd still risk inadvertently leaving someone out like Michael, who held down the fort for two years while I was deep in bookland.

Finally, I dedicate this work to all the brave exposers and seekers of truth.

I got up to 100 words per minute!

Mom & Dad

ABOUT THE AUTHOR

Valerie Naiman is an authority on living on the edge. She says that's where the most vibrant life is. She is an adoptee, author, singer, songwriter, ontologist, environmentalist, ecovillage founder, spiritual travel guide, beekeeper, and a mama to her dwarf goats. She's probably a Gemini, although her birth date is unknown.

Valerie holds a Master of Arts from the University of Miami, a Doctorate of Divinity from ULC, and has been a certified permaculture designer for 33 years.

Naiman is the president of the Spiritual Growth Foundation, a 501c3 NPO where she's served for over 30 years. Much of that work has been supporting disenfranchised children at home and abroad in India where she lived for 11 years.

Valerie was an actress turned costume designer for NBC and films in NY, CA, and Miami during the 1970s. In 1980, she moved to Asheville, NC and opened the first costume shop and balloon delivery business in the region. By the mid 80's she turned to working with indigenous wisdom keepers around the world, leading tours to sacred sites in the USA and abroad. In 1990 she had a vision that ended in founding Earthaven Ecovillage, the first permaculture-designed village in North America.

Mystic Masquerade, An Adoptee's Search for Truth, was compiled from journals she wrote during decades of her biological and spiritual search.

Valerie now lives in Asheville, NC with her honeybees and dwarf goats.

Connect with Valerie

Visit my website at *http://valerienaiman.com/* to get freebies, hear podcasts, listen to audiobooks, story songs, and more.

Do you want to see photos of some of the stories in my book, or get tools for searching? I'd love to share more with you and it will warm my heart to hear about your experience reading my book.

I'm offering a perk of a free phone consultation about living on the edge or talking about how my book affected you. Email me at *valerie@valerienaiman.com* if you'd like to take me up on my offer.

COMING SOON

Story-Songs for Adoptees and the Triad.mp3

Books in the hopper:

The Making of Earthaven Ecovillage

Walk-ins... Are they Real?

SUBSCRIBE ON MY WEBSITE FOR UPDATES